T0326605

Job Interview Corpus

Daniela Wawra

Job Interview Corpus

Data Transcription and Major Topics in Corpus Linguistics

PETER LANG
EDITION

Bibliographic Information published by the Deutsche Nationalbibliothek
The Deutsche Nationalbibliothek lists this publication in the Deutsche Nationalbibliografie; detailed bibliographic data is available in the internet at http://dnb.d-nb.de.

Library of Congress Cataloging-in-Publication Data
Wawra, Daniela.
Job interview corpus : data transcription and major topics in corpus linguistics / Daniela Wawra.
pages cm
Includes bibliographical references.
ISBN 978-3-631-65402-6 — ISBN 978-3-653-04431-7 (ebook) 1. Employment interviewing. 2. Corpora (Linguistics) I. Title.
HF5549.5.I6W39 2014
658.3'1124—dc23

2014036085

ISBN 978-3-631-65402-6 (Print)
E-ISBN 978-3-653-04431-7 (E-Book)
DOI 10.3726/978-3-653-04431-7

© Peter Lang GmbH
Internationaler Verlag der Wissenschaften
Frankfurt am Main 2014
All rights reserved.
Peter Lang Edition is an Imprint of Peter Lang GmbH.

Peter Lang – Frankfurt am Main · Bern · Bruxelles · New York · Oxford · Warszawa · Wien

This publication has been peer reviewed.

www.peterlang.com

Contents

1. Introduction

> Perhaps the greatest single event in the history of linguistics was the invention of the tape recorder, which for the first time has captured natural conversation and made it accessible to systematic study. (Halliday 1994: xxiii)

> Spoken corpora provide a unique resource for the exploration of naturally occurring discourse; and the growing interest in the development of spoken corpora is testament to the value they provide to a diverse number of research communities. (Adolphs/Carter 2013: 5)

The aim of this book with its accompanying audio files is to make accessible a corpus of 40 authentic English job interviews. This would not have been possible without the consent of the interviewees to be recorded for research purposes. Thus, I am very much indebted to all of them and would like to thank them for their valuable support in my undertaking. Moreover, it was a great pleasure to meet and get to know each and every one of them during the course of the interviews.

The transcriptions of the interviews published here can be used by students, teachers and researchers alike for linguistic analyses of spoken discourse and as authentic material for language learning in the classroom. Various possibilities of using corpora in the classroom are, for example, sketched by Sinclair (2004), Mauranen (2004: 89–105), Bennett (2010), in the sections V "Using a corpus for language pedagogy and methodology" and VI "Designing corpus-based materials for the language classroom" of *The Routledge Handbook of Corpus Linguistics* (O'Keeffe/McCarthy (eds.) 2010), by Flowerdew (2012: 208–224) and Reppen (2012: 204–213). The benefits of using corpora in language learning contexts are summarized by Bennett (2010: 93), who states that "[a]*ll language skills can be taught using corpora*" and that "[u]*sing corpora can provide a unique element of learning to your classroom*". She goes on:

> (...) using corpora in the classroom can certainly facilitate language acquisition. More effective classroom materials engage learners in actual language use and in a variety of registers, which ultimately leads to increased motivation and more targeted learning. Used in conjunction with other materials (textbooks) and teaching approaches, corpora provide learners with the tools needed for language acquisition. (Bennett 2010: 93)

I started the recording and transcription of the job interviews while I was working on a project concerning the language use of women and men.[1] The first eighteen interviews were used for an empirical study of the sexes' language use in the context of the job interview. Its results are published in Wawra (2004). I became interested in the discourse genre 'job interview' because I believed this to be an area which would lead to major consequences for job applicants of either sex if their language use was preventing them from getting the job. While looking for research in the field, I was surprised to discover that there were almost no linguistic studies concerning job interviews. The few studies that had been done contained no authentic material at all or only a very small number of interviews.[2] However, particularly when studying job interviews, it is essential that we analyze authentic data and not the simulated conversations of mock interviews. The linguistic behavior of the applicants is likely to differ when they know that nothing is at stake and that the interview is in no way significant for their future lives. There are several reasons why up until now so few authentic interviews have been studied by linguists: One being that the job interview constitutes a very sensitive communication situation in which interviewers and applicants usually do not like to be observed. Since there are no universal rules as to how to conduct a job interview, interviewers fear they might be criticized by the researcher for their way of carrying it out. In the worst case they could be blamed for discriminating against certain individuals. Interviewers also fear that the applicant could be irritated by the presence of an observer and not behave in the same way as they would do without. Ultimately, interviewers do not want to risk being sued by applicants who did not get the job in the end, a possible argument being that they were not able to present themselves and their qualifications adequately due to the presence of the observer. This alone is reason enough to object to requests of researchers asking to record job interviews. On

---

1 Wawra, Daniela. 2004. *Männer und Frauen im Job Interview: Eine evolutionspsychologische Studie zu ihrem Sprachgebrauch im Englischen*. Münster. (The study explores the sexes' language use in general and in the context of the job interview in particular).
2 For an overview of linguistic studies on job interviews and more information on them see Wawra (2004:171).

part of the applicants, very much is at stake during a job interview, their future depends on it and they reveal much about themselves – personally and professionally. Therefore, it seems natural that some applicants might not be enthusiastic about another stranger being present in such a situation, someone who is not involved, learns much about them and causes them to be even more nervous than they already are.[3]

I was finally able to circumvent these problems when I was in a position to offer real jobs as English phonetics tutors to exchange students with English as a native language at the University of Passau. With the consent of the interviewees I was able to tape authentic job interviews without any third party having to be present as an observer. I decided against video- and opted for audiotaping, as the latter could be done without drawing much of the applicants' attention to it and thus not distracting them from the task at hand. Thanks to this arrangement, I managed to record 40 authentic job interviews. Still, the task required patience, since I only interviewed those exchange students that were genuinely interested in getting the job. During some of the semesters I interviewed only three or four students which is why it took three and a half years for a corpus of this size to be compiled.

The following section 2 provides a short introduction to corpus linguistics. Major characteristics of corpora will be discussed and different kinds of corpora will be introduced, including a classification of the job interview corpus. Section 3 will outline major characteristics of the discourse genre 'job interview'. Section 4, then, contains more detailed information on the job interview corpus published in this book. Section 5 explains the transcription conventions used. You will find a bibliography in section 6 and section 7, finally, contains the transcriptions of the 40 job interviews.

---

3 cf. also Wawra (2004: 172) for a discussion of the obstacles researchers encounter when they want to study authentic job interviews.

2. Corpus Linguistics

2.1 What is corpus linguistics? Setting the scene

Corpus linguistics, in the sense of searching for words and indexing them in a text, has its roots in the 13th century when scholars applied these processes to the Christian Bible (cf. McCarthy/O'Keeffe 2010: 3). According to McCarthy/ O'Keeffe (2010: 4), the American structuralists in the 1950s were "forerunners" of corpus linguists "in the sense of data gathering (…) [and] in terms of the commitment to putting real language data at the core of what linguists study". However, the beginnings of corpus linguistics in this sense can be traced back even further, at least to the beginning of the 20th century and the work of Leonard Bloomfield (cf. Bloomfield 1917, Emons 1997: 63). The impact of corpus linguistics since then has been "enormous, transforming both how we understand and how we study language across a range of different areas" (Hyland/Huat/Handford 2012: 3). Corpora added

> an empirical dimension to language studies, which was not possible before, or not possible to the same extent, allowing researchers to replace intuitions, strengthen interpretations, reinforce claims and generally talk about language with greater confidence. While corpora themselves do not provide new information about language, the ability to draw on large samples of naturally occurring data allows analysts to offer enhanced descriptions of language and how it works (…). The pace of this change has also been considerable, accelerated by the growing accessibility and processing capabilities of computers (…). (Hyland/Huat/Handford 2012: 3)

Corpus linguistics has mostly been described as a methodology and not as a separate discipline of linguistics such as phonetics/phonology, morphology/ word-formation, semantics or syntax, for example (as suggested by Tognini-Bonelli 2001: 1, cf. also Curzan 2012: 11 and McEnery/Hardie 2012: 1). While these subdisciplines of linguistics "describe, or explain, a certain aspect of language", "[c]orpus linguistics (…) is not restricted to a particular aspect of language. Rather, it can be employed to explore almost any area of linguistic research" (McEnery et al. 2006: 7; cf. also Mindt 2009: 7). McEnery/Hardie (2012: 1) define corpus linguistics "as dealing with some set of machine-readable texts which is deemed an appropriate basis on which to study a specific set of research questions". In corpus linguistics we thus usually deal with large sets of data and have to rely largely on automated tools that search through the data efficiently, i.e. thoroughly and quickly (cf. McEnery/Hardie 2012: 2). Within the field of corpus linguistics a distinction has been made between **corpus-based** and **corpus-driven** studies (cf. Mindt (2009: 69–88) for a comparison of the application of the two approaches):

> Corpus-based studies typically use corpus data in order to explore a theory or hypothesis, typically one established in the current literature, in order to validate it, refute it or refine it. The definition of corpus linguistics as a method underpins this approach (...). Corpus-driven linguistics rejects the characterisation of corpus linguistics as a method and claims instead that the corpus itself should be the sole source of our hypotheses about language. (McEnery/Hardie 2012: 6)

Corpus-driven approaches are closely associated with "Neo-Firthian" corpus linguistics (McEnery/Hardie 2012: 6, 122, 147–152). They take a "'corpus-as-theory'" stance and reject the usage of any "theoretical concepts that pre-exist their encounter with the corpus (...). (...) any explanation of language patterns [must] derive directly from the analyst's interaction with the data" (McEnery/Hardie 2012: 148). The job interview corpus has been compiled to test hypotheses on men's and women's language use in the context of the job interview. The study was thus a **corpus-based** one that is rooted in the "'corpus-as-method' tradition" which

> considers corpora and corpus techniques to be sources of empirical data that may be deployed in support or refutation of any explanatory theory about language – even a theory devised in whole or in part without reference to corpus data. (McEnery/Hardie 2012: 148)

Meanwhile, the methodology of corpus linguistics transcends its original field: Its techniques have also been used and adopted in other disciplines (cf. Kytö 2012: 1; Curzan 2012, 11), culminating in the recent establishment of the field 'Digital Humanities' (cf. e.g. McEnery/Hardie 2012: 231–233). Curzan (2012, 10), for example, emphasizes the great potential of corpus linguistics for cross-disciplinary cooperation when it comes to "exploiting large electronic text databases".

2.2 What is a corpus? Defining features and problems

Before it was used in linguistics, the term 'corpus' had been used already in the 18th century "to refer to a collection or binding together of written works of a similar nature (…), so that scholars might refer to a 'corpus of the Latin poets'" (McCarthy/O'Keeffe 2010: 5). In the context of linguistics, a 'corpus' was probably first defined in 1956 as "the body of written or spoken material upon which a linguistic analysis is based" (McCarthy/ O'Keeffe 2010: 5). More generally, it has also frequently been defined as "a body of naturally occurring language" (McEnery et al. 2006: 4) or "a collection of texts" (Tognini-Bonelli 2010: 18). In our digital age, a corpus is sometimes defined as "any electronic collection of text" (Curzan 2012: 12). Corpora are usually "assembled with particular purposes in mind, and (…) to be (…) representative of some language or text type" (Leech 1992: 116). From the many definitions, McEnery et al. (2006: 5) (cf. also McEnery/ Hardie 2012: 1–2) extract the following features researchers mostly agree on as defining a corpus: It is

- "a collection of" texts that are
- "*machine-readable*"
- "*sampled*"
- "*authentic*"
- "*representative*".

Here, "text" refers to written and spoken language that has been transcribed.[4] Nowadays, "*machine-readable*" means that the language data compiled in a corpus can be processed with the help of a computer. "*Sampled*" data have been collected for a specific research purpose and have not been compiled randomly. A corpus "is typically a sample of a much larger population" (McEnery et al. 2006: 19). However, researchers often do not agree on which sampling techniques are most appropriate to reach the set goals of an empirical study.[5] Corpora are further used to describe actual or "real life" language use (cf. McEnery 2006: 2–5; Curzan 2012, 11) and to study "how speakers and writers use language to achieve various communicative goals" (McEnery 2006: 5). Does "actual" equal "authentic"? One of the synonyms the Collins Cobuild Advanced Dictionary (CCAD)

---

4   More precisely, Halliday/Hasan define "text" as follows: "The word TEXT is used in linguistics to refer to any passage, spoken or written, of whatever length, that does form a unified whole" (Halliday/Hasan ⁶1984: 1).
5   For an overview of different sampling techniques see e.g., Meyer (2002: 43).

(2009) gives for "authentic" is "genuine" and the latter is defined as "real and not pretended" and in this sense it can be regarded as synonymous with "actual", which is defined as "real or genuine". The language data compiled in corpora are thus not made up but occurred in reality. However, would we still speak of authentic data if certain language use occurred "for real" in, for example, a mock interview, that is, in a situation that has been artificially created? The language used in such a situation is "real", but the situation is not. Would this, therefore, make the language used "un-"authentic? There is another definition cited for "authentic" in the CCAD (2009): "such a good imitation that it is almost the same as or as good as the original". Are the linguistic data of a mock interview "almost the same as or as good as" the ones we could obtain in a real interview? In this respect, the question whether data are "authentic" or not, can be difficult to answer. If we apply a definition of authenticity that I will term 'strong authenticity claim', we would reject the claim that imitations – no matter how close they are to the original – are authentic. If we make a strong authenticity claim for linguistic data, this would then mean that the situation or context of the communication *and* the language use would have to be genuine or real. However, most researchers would probably also use the term 'corpus' for a compilation of mock interviews, and we could still call these authentic if we make a 'weak authenticity claim': Although the situation or context of the communication is not real for the participants, their language use is genuine or real in this artificially set up situation. Another example is dictionaries. They, too, often advertise that they contain authentic language use. However, the examples cited have often been edited and adapted to the purpose of providing clearer examples for the use of a certain word for language learners. Thus, the Collins Cobuild Advanced Dictionary (CCAD) (2009), for example, claims:

AUTHENTIC SAMPLES FROM CORPUS (back of front cover)

Cobuild's original undertaking to help learners with <u>real</u> English continues to underpin our approach. The Collins Bank of English ® **corpus** has grown to 654 million words. It contains up-to-date English language from thousands of different written and spoken sources. As ever, the corpus lies at the heart of each entry, helping lexicographers to make confident and accurate decisions about the different senses of a word, the language of the definition, the choice of examples, and the grammatical information given. (CCAD 2009: xi)

Then, they continue, however:

Examples themselves remain close to the corpus, with minor changes made so that they are more successful as dictionary examples. (CCAD 2009: xi)

The data used in the CCAD (2009) would, therefore, also be authentic only according to the weak authenticity claim: The linguistic data used are "almost the same as or as good as the original" or – as in the context of dictionaries, for example – the changed data are even better for the purpose of making a certain point (usually, in the case of dictionaries this is to make the usage of a word clearer). **The job interview data assembled in the corpus in this book, then, are authentic data, according to the strong authenticity claim.**

The question, finally, when a corpus can be considered as representative, has been much debated (see, for example, the answers to the question, how representative a corpus can be in Viana/Zyngier/Barnbrook 2011). Again, I would like to start with a dictionary definition. The Collins Cobuild Advanced Dictionary (2009) defines "representative" as "[s]omeone [or something] who [or which] is typical of the group to which they belong", while "typical" is described as "someone or something that shows the most usual characteristics of a particular type of person or thing [or behaviour], and is therefore a good example of that type". What would be considered the "most usual characteristics"? What is most "usual" is "what happens or what is done most often in a particular situation", according to the Collins dictionary definition. Leech (1991: 27) considers a corpus to be representative of the variety of language it is to represent if the results of the corpus study can be generalized in terms of this variety of language. According to Biber (1993: 243), "[r]epresentativeness refers to the extent to which a sample includes the full range of variability in a population". McEnery/Hardie (2012: 10) state that representativeness is an "ideal[ ], which corpus builders strive for but rarely, if ever, attain. (…) [It is a] matter[ ] of degree". If we sum up these definitions and try to get closer to the **concept of representativeness for linguistic corpora**, we could say that it relates to

- **goodness-of-example:** The language use that is a good example for the communication situation or variety that is the object of the study, is representative for it.

- **typicality:** The language use that is typical for the communication situation is representative for it.
- **frequency:** Language variables that occur most frequently in the communication situation or variety are the most "usual" or "typical" ones and are thus representative for it.
- **generalization:** The linguistic variables can be considered as representative for the regional or social language variety they are to represent if they also occur most frequently in other comparable communication situations.
- **the full range of variability:** If all linguistic variables that can possibly occur in the communication situation under study, occur in the corpus, it is representative.

In the end, however, the question of whether a corpus comes close to being representative or not can only be answered if we look at the "ultimate use of the corpus": "To create a valid and representative corpus, it is important (...), to plan the construction carefully before the collection of data even begins" (Meyer 2002: 53). "The research question one has in mind when building (or thinking of using) a corpus defines its representativeness" (McEnery et al. 2006: 18; cf. also Adolphs/Carter 2013: 7). As a user of an already existing corpus, it is important to make sure that the corpus is suitable for the planned research task (cf. also McEnery/Hardie 2012: 11). If we combine all these attempts in order to come closer to the concept of representativeness, the job interview corpus published here can, at least, cautiously, be regarded as representative of the speech of male and female students in job interviews with regard to certain variables of speech. Some of these have been identified with the help of statistical tests used in a study I conducted involving the first 18 interviews of this corpus. The results of the statistical tests are published in Wawra (2004: 284–340). For some of the linguistic variables there were not enough instances in the corpus of 18 interviews so that the results of the empirical studies were not significant. The enlargement of the corpus is very likely to have increased its representativeness in this area of study (the comparison of male and female language use). An open question is, whether or not the job interview corpus can be regarded as a sample of the larger population – men and women in general – and whether or not the significant results of the study on differences in the subject's language use can be generalized. In order to obtain a definite answer, further comparable studies of authentic job interviews with individuals of all ages and social and professional backgrounds would be needed. Still, it should always be kept in mind that, following Meyer (2012: 40), "any corpus will have its limitations".

2.3 What kinds of corpora are there and where does the job interview corpus belong? An overview

The following major **types of corpora** can be distinguished (the following features are taken from Meyer 2002: 22–24, McEnery 2006: 59–70 and McEnery/Hardie 2012: 3, Dahlmann/Adolphs 2012: 125):

- general vs. specialized
- multi-purpose vs. specialized purpose
- written vs. spoken
- monolingual/-modal vs. multilingual/-modal
- synchronic vs. diachronic/historical
- annotated and unannotated
- learner, parallel, monitor, sample

If a corpus is general, "it will typically be balanced with regard to the genres and domains that typically represent the language under consideration" (McEnery et al. 2006: 59). "Balanced" means that the corpus has to cover "a wide variety of frequent and important text categories that are proportionally sampled from the target population" (Meyer 2002: 21). General corpora can also be called multi-purpose corpora when one wants to emphasize that they can "be used for a variety of different purposes (...). For this reason, each of these corpora contains a broad range of genres" (Meyer 2002: 36). Among such various purposes these corpora could be used for are studies of English grammar and vocabulary, differences between genres or language varieties (cf. Meyer 2002: 36). In contrast, **the corpus of English job interviews in this book is a specialized corpus** as it is restricted to a special genre, in this case, job interviews, and to a specific social group, here, university students. It has been compiled for a particular or **specialized purpose**: Looking into the language use of male and female students. The English job interview corpus contains transcribed spoken language and is, thus, a **spoken corpus**. While

> [d]atabases for the study of written language run into millions of words (...), [y]et there are still relatively few projects devoted to spoken corpus linguistics. (Adolphs/Carter 2013: 1)

This is certainly due to the fact that it is very "time-consuming to gather and transcribe" spoken language data (if you cannot draw on transcribed spoken discourse of political speeches or news broadcasts from the World Wide Web, for example)[6] (McEnery/Hardie 2012: 4). So far, the spoken corpora are usually "**monomodal**", i.e. they only comprise verbal communication (Adolphs/Carter 2013: 1). However, the first spoken corpora that "align audio and visual data streams with the transcript of a conversation" have already been developed (Adolphs/Knight 2010: 39) (see Adolphs/ Knight 2010: 38–39 also for a general overview of spoken corpora). As "[c]ommunication processes are multimodal in nature", I agree with Adolphs/Carter (2013: 1) who demand "more multimodal spoken corpora by integrating textual, prosodic and gestural representations". If we define verbal communication as monomodal, as Adolphs/Carter (2013: 1) do (see above), the job interview corpus is monomodal. If, however, a monomodal corpus is defined as containing only one mode of communication, e.g. written language, then the job interview data included here could be described as multimodal inasmuch as the transcription of the job interviews is accompanied – if not aligned – by audio files, which allow for the study of prosody (cf. e.g. Dahlmann/Adolphs 2012: 125, Kratochvílová/ Wolf 2010: 12 for such a concept of monomodality). The job interview corpus is clearly **monolingual** as it is limited to one language, i.e. English (although it contains a few German words) (cf. McEnery/Hardie 2012: 18). It is **synchronic** as the data were collected within a relatively short time span (three and a half years) in which no major changes occurred in the way that English was used. It does not contain data from different time periods (cf. McEnery et al. 2006: 65) that would lend themselves to historically comparative analyses. The corpus is **unannotated,** i.e. "linguistic

---

6   Whether such data are reliable and useful, however, depends on your research question (cf. McEnery/Hardie 2012: 4).

analyses are [not] encoded in the corpus data itself", nor is the corpus accompanied by a "'stand-off' annotation", i.e. annotations are neither "stored separately (…) [nor] linked in to the data" (McEnery/Hardie 2012: 13). The job interview corpus is not a learner corpus in that it does not include written or spoken discourse of second language learners (cf. McEnery et al. 2006: 65). The corpus is neither a parallel nor a monitor corpus as it neither contains comparable data of language use in job interviews in another language nor is it constantly "updated" – that is to say, "supplemented with fresh material and keeps increasing in size, though the proportion of text types included in the corpus remains constant" (McEnery et al. 2006: 67; cf. also McEnery/Hardie 2012: 6–7). Hence, it is not dynamic, a feature which a monitor corpus would have to exhibit. The job interview corpus can therefore best be classified as a **sample corpus**, as it tries "to be *balanced* and *representative* within a particular *sampling frame* which defines the type of language, the *population*, that we would like to characterise" (McEnery/Hardie 2012: 8). More precisely, the job interview corpus can be described as a "**snapshot corpus**" within this category, as it "represents a 'snapshot'" (McEnery/Hardie 2012: 9) of the language use of 17 male and 23 female university students with English as a native language within a limited time frame (2001–2004).

The Internet, which is nowadays often used as a corpus, is sometimes classified as a separate type of corpus. This is commonly described as the "*Web as Corpus*" approach (cf. e.g. McEnery/Hardie 2012: 7; see Lew (2012: 289–300), for example, for a short critical discussion of its pros and cons). The terms Internet and Web are often used as synonyms. However, strictly speaking, the Internet is the more general term which also comprises E-Mail, for example (cf. Hoffmann 2009: 24).[7] McEnery/Hardie (2012: 7) describe the "concept of *Web as Corpus*" as being "very similar in many ways to the idea of the monitor corpus". It was not included here

---

7   Hoffmann (2009: 24) states: "*Internet* refers to the global network that is made up of smaller interconnected computer networks. (…) the *World Wide Web*, which consists of a system of interlinked hypertexts, is only one of the many services available on the Internet. Other examples of Internet services – which rely on different communication protocols – are electronic mail, Usenet and online chat".

as a separate kind of corpus, however, as the Internet can also be seen as an immense data source which lends itself to various data collection regimes that can provide *all* of the types of corpora cited above. From this perspective, the Internet is what could be called a **hyper-corpus**, in analogy to the relation between a hyperonym and its hyponyms in semantics.[8]

2.4 Corpus linguistics as a means to an end

Corpus linguistics should always be "a means to an end rather than an end in itself" (McCarthy/O'Keeffe 2010: 7). Especially in times when there are ever more and ever better developed tools available to us for doing corpus linguistic work, there is a danger that we could be tempted to analyse data in certain ways simply because we can. In accordance with the functionalists, corpus linguistic work is at its best when it takes into account that

> [l]anguage is not (...) an abstract, isolated system, but one that is *used* to communicate meaning, and which is shaped by the ways it is used, by the contexts in which it occurs and by the structure of human cognition. (McEnery/Hardie 2012: 168).

"[L]inguistic items (...) [thus constitute] 'discursive, professional and/or social practices'" (Hunston 2012: 242) and we should remind ourselves that the

> social and cultural world that we as human beings inhabit exists, and is expressed and recorded, to a very large degree by means of language. (...) So it can be said that experience of the human world is largely a textually mediated experience, and, to that extent, human beings live in a textually mediated world. (McEnery/Hardie 2012: 230).

Linguistic studies that are based on the analysis of corpora should therefore "not stop at the description of (...) texts" but rather also include

---

8 Hoffmann (2009: 24) distinguishes between the three following major possibilities of how to use the Internet as corpus: (1) as a whole ("'Internet as corpus' approach"), where the Internet or "more typically" the Web "is considered as a single, huge corpus"; (2) as a random subset ("'mega-corpus/mini-Internet' approach"), where a "subset" of the Internet is investigated, which is "a smaller version of the whole: the contents of the corpus are randomly selected in order to mirror the contents of the full corpus on a smaller scale"; (3) as a sampled subset ("'Internet as corpus shop' approach"), where "the contents [of the subset corpus] are selected on the basis of certain criteria to contain specific types of language use" such as "newspaper texts", for example.

an analysis of "the contexts of the texts' production and consumption" as well as their functions and "locate the linguistic study firmly within a broader social context" (Hunston 2012: 242). Let us now take a closer look at the discourse genre 'job interview'.

3. The discourse genre 'job interview'[9]

A job interview may be classified as a subcategory of the discourse genre 'interview', which can be characterized as follows:

> An interview is purposeful, whereas a conversation may not be. Interviewers must draw out the desired information while motivating the interviewee to cooperate. Because the interview has a predetermined purpose, it is more formal than a conversation. Interviews are clearly structured. They are comprised of an opening, a body, and a closing, and the participants have specific roles. In contrast, many conversations appear formless. Conversations may involve an exchange of information, but the exchange is a universal and essential characteristic of the interview. (Lahiff/Penrose [5]1997: 484f)

All this applies to job interviews. What is their specific situational context?

> The term SITUATION, meaning the 'context of situation' in which a text is embedded, refers to all those extra-linguistic factors which have some bearing on the text itself. (Halliday/Hasan [6]1984: 21)[10]

Among the "extra-linguistic factors" that Halliday/Hasan refer to and that have an influence on language use are, in a wider sense, the cultural and institutional structures the interview is embedded in. The cultural structures provide the knowledge of which behavior is appropriate when interacting with people. The institutional structures define the duties of the members of the institution (cf. Komter 1987: 201). Job interviews take place in institutional contexts and the language used in job interviews has been defined as institutional discourse. Discourse is institutional when one or more discourse participants represent a formal organization. In addition, the discourse must have a certain purpose which is related to the larger goals of the institution (cf. Drew/Heritage 1992: 22; Geluykens/Pelsmaekers 1999: 8). The purpose of a job interview is to find the candidate that is best suited for an open job position (cf. Lahiff/Penrose [5]1997: 490). In this sense, the job interview is a "gatekeeping encounter", such as tests or interviews to allocate social support:

---

9   What follows is mainly taken from Wawra (2004: 172–175).
10 "Text" is defined here as follows: "The word TEXT is used in linguistics to refer to any passage, spoken or written, of whatever length, that does form a unified whole" (Halliday/Hasan [6]1984: 1).

These 'people sorting institutions' distribute goods, services or life-chances. They can be seen as forms of social guardianship that allocates, awards or adjudicates on the basis of the professional judgements of the supervisors. (...) In all gatekeeping encounters talk is an important vehicle for the business at hand. All gatekeeping encounters involve a conflict of interests, as one party is subjected to the judgements of the other party. The expertise of the gatekeepers, as well as their reference to standards derived from extra-individual, cultural structures, may serve as conflict reduction or control. Gatekeeping encounters only work when the participants believe in the system, and can thus be seen as important means for legitimating the justice of selections. (Komter 1987: 204f)

The job interview as a specific subcategory of gatekeeping encounters is usually characterized by a dyadic composition: Two persons or, better, two parties, the interviewee on the one side and the party representing the institution on the other side. The latter can consist of one or more people. Typically, the distribution of status or roles is asymmetric: The interviewer is in a dominant position, while the interviewee has a subordinate role. This is because the interviewer has something the interviewee wants: a job. And the interviewer has the power to grant or deny the interviewee his wish to get the job.

Job interviews usually have a ritual character; they are clearly structured (cf. Komter 1987: 203). This again reflects the asymmetric relationship of the two parties. The following five phases have been described as typical (cf. Auer 1998: 10):

1. Small Talk
2. Information on the job and the institution
3. Information on the applicant
4. Information on administrative details
5. Small talk

The interviewer determines the form of the interaction, whereas the applicant has to adapt (cf. Komter 1987: 12). The typical interaction format of the job interview consists of question – answer sequences (cf. Komter 1987: 202; Bogaers 1998: 38).

The basic purpose of the job interview is to exchange information (cf. Komter 1987: 203). The interviewer has information on the open position, the job's "profile" (vgl. Komter 1987: 199). They want to elicit as much information as possible about the interviewee in order to find out whether the applicant is suited for the job. The applicant's aptitude is judged in relation to the job profile. There is a conflict of interests between the two parties: The interviewer wants to reveal possible weaknesses of the applicant with regard to the requirements of the job. The applicant, in contrast, wishes to conceal those weaknesses (cf. Komter 1987: 204f). By making use of certain strategic moves, the interviewer can try to elicit information which shows that the applicant is not suited for the job. The strategic power of the interviewers is based on their better knowledge of the job requirements and conditions and on the fact that they can judge the applicant according to the qualifications they consider to be most important for the job. This official, explicit agenda of the job interview, namely, to obtain information on the qualifications of the applicant for the open position, is expanded by the implicit goal to judge the personality of the applicant:

> (...) viewed in this way, the explicit agenda is just the means for solving the underlying problems of the implicit agenda. (vgl. Adelswärd 1988: 56)

Both parties, interviewer(s) and applicant alike, are aware of this implicit agenda. Applicants know that they must present themselves as advantageously as possible to get the job (cf. Auer 1998: 10). The interviewer obtains information about the applicant by what he says but also by how he presents himself (cf. Komter 1987: 136). This comprises verbal and non-verbal communication (gestures, facial expressions, body composure ...) (cf. e.g. Lahiff/Penrose [5]1997: 381–397 for an overview of major characteristics of non-verbal communication). The transcribed job interviews in this book concentrate on verbal and some features of paraverbal communication: what was said and how was it said (cf. Lahiff/Penrose [5]1997: 382f).

4. The job interview corpus

The job interviews were conducted in April and October 2001, October 2003, April 2004, and October 2004 at the University of Passau, Germany, with 17 male and 23 female exchange students from Great Britain, Ireland, the United States, and Australia. The interviews were audio-taped and comprise about 425 minutes of recording time altogether. You will find information on the age, sex and origins of the interviewees at the beginning of the respective interviews in section 7. The interviews are authentic: They were conducted to find students with English as a native language for the job of a phonetics tutor. Only exchange students who confirmed their interest in the post were invited to an interview. The phonetics tutorials were an accompanying class to an introductory course on English phonetics and phonology at the University of Passau. In these tutorials the English native speakers were to conduct practical pronunciation exercises with the German students to help them improve their pronunciation in English. The tutors were to teach four hours a week and they were paid € 160 per month. The interviewer was the author of this book and teacher of the introductory class on English phonetics and phonology.

Prior to compiling a list of interview questions, a job profile was worked out. It contains major practical and social requirements that a phonetics tutor should have:

Practical requirements for the job of a phonetics tutor:[11]
1. clear, correct articulation in English[12]
2. good rhetorical abilities
3. teaching experience
4. experience in teaching pronunciation
5. theoretical knowledge about English phonetics and phonology
6. a good ear for pronunciation mistakes
7. thorough
8. diligent

---

11 See also Wawra (2004: 177).

12 The varieties of *American, British, Australian, Irish and Scottish English* are represented in the interviews. The applicants were expected to have a correct standard pronunciation in their respective variety.

Social requirements for the job of a phonetics tutor:
1. openness in dealing with people 2. patient 3. friendly 4. cooperative/suited for teamwork[13] 5. communicative 6. reliable 7. responsible 8. helpful

This job profile was to make sure that the interview questions would reveal as much as possible about the aptitude of the candidates for the job. Based on this profile and compilations of frequently asked questions in job interviews (cf. e.g. Biegeleisen, J. I. 1994: 61–68), the following list of interview questions was developed:

Interview questions[14]
1. Tell me a little bit about yourself: Where do you come from and what studies have you done so far? 2. Why did you choose to study in Germany? 3. Which qualifications will help you with your job as a tutor? 4. Which personal qualifications will help you with the job? 5. What are your strengths / weaknesses? 6. What aspect of the job interests you most / least? 7. Do you prefer to work independently or with others? 8. When you recognize that your students are in a bad mood and uncooperative — how do you deal with it? 9. How do you handle criticism? 10. How do you feel about speaking in public? Do you have any relevant experience that would help you in a public speaking role? 11. All things considered, are you confident you can handle this job? 12. Do you have any questions?

All applicants were asked the same interview questions in the same order. This is in accordance with the guidelines of the Equal Employment Opportunity Commission which state that all candidates should be asked the same

---

13 This competence was important as the phonetics tutor was to cooperate with a German native speaker who taught the students phonetic transcription.
14 See also Wawra (2004: 178).

questions in a job interview to ensure equal treatment and comparability (cf. Lahiff/Penrose [5]1997: 490). In the transcription of the interviews, the numbers (1–12) refer to the above questions. The interviews are "closed" or "standardized" interviews, in other words, the order and wording of the questions were determined in advance and followed by the interviewer (cf. Sellien/Sellien [14]1997: 2018). Only the last question – "Do you have any questions?" – provided an opportunity for the applicants to raise topics themselves. Therefore, monologs or "single-party talk" which Edelsky also describes as "floor F1" (Edelsky 1981; 383f, 416), are predominant in the interviews (and the rare additional discourse contributions of the interviewer were usually not transcribed). This interview style is to be classified as "highly directive":

> In the **highly directive interviewing style,** the interviewer exerts strong control. Typically, little time is devoted to establishing rapport. Most of the questions are closed, and the responses elicited are often recorded. The highly directive style is frequently used for gathering factual information. Many, if not all, of the questions asked by the highly directive interviewer may be prepared in advance. (Lahiff/Penrose [5]1997: 495)

Finally, it is to be noted that the typical five phases of a job interview described above could also be observed in the interviews published here. However, only phase 3 – information on the interviewee – was transcribed, as this was the one most relevant to the research project that the job interview corpus was originally compiled for.[15]

---

15 See also Wawra (2004: 178f).

5. Transcription conventions[16]

There is no transcription system that could render precisely each and every small detail of spoken language. There is not *one* unified transcription system to render spoken discourse. Such a unified transcription system could never adequately represent the different contexts with all their peculiarities in which spoken discourse can occur. Therefore, the transcription system needs to be adapted to the respective context in which the spoken discourse occurs and to the peculiarities of the speech situation. Nevertheless, whatever system you choose, it will remain deficient. The closest you can get to the 'real' spoken discourse is by means of a recording which, however, still is just an incomplete re-presentation of the original interview in a new context. With the transcription system used here, two major goals were in the foreground:

1. The transcription of the job interviews should be as adequate as possible to render the spoken discourse.
2. The transcription should be as simple as possible to make it easily readable.

To reach these goals different conventions from several transcription systems were combined and some conventions were added by the author that seemed important for a close representation of the interviews. Depending on what your research goals are, however, the transcriptions might not be detailed enough for you, particularly with regard to pronunciation and prosodic aspects. Therefore, you might want to go through the recordings of the interviews and work out such aspects in more detail. The transcriptions you will find here represent the interviews in their basic and major aspects. They are a compromise between readability and particularity and will make it easier to look into more specific aspects of the spoken discourse and start with detailed research questions.

The major part of the transcription conventions are based on Eggins/ Slade (1997: 1–5). The different kinds of intonation that they distinguish were rendered with the help of intonation analysis according to Halliday

---

16 What follows is mainly taken from Wawra (2004: 248–250).

(1994: 302–304) and they are rendered with punctuation. The designations of text and speaker are taken from Quirk/Svartvik (1980: 21–25), the labels 'male' and 'female' were added. The convention of italic print was taken from Lenz (1989: 256). The last three conventions (under the heading "Other transcription conventions") were added by the author. What follows now is a listing and an explanation of the transcription conventions used.

Designation of text and speaker

I 1f, 1   The letter 'I' stands for 'Interview'; the following numbers from 1 to 40 refer to each interviewee, respectively; 'f' or 'm' indicates the sex of the speaker – female or male. The number after the comma refers to the number of the question that was answered (1–12).

Punctuation to render intonation

Periods   .   mark prosodic completion (independent of whether a statement is grammatically complete) or security that is usually marked by falling intonation (this corresponds to Halliday's (1994: 302) *tone 1*). It is implicated here that it will indicate incompleteness or insecurity when there is no full stop at the end of a turn as the contribution to the communication fades.

Commas   ,   indicate the speaker's segmentation of non-final speech. They are also used to ease readability of longer passages.

Question marks   ?   indicate questions or insecurity (this is often connected to rising intonation and corresponds to Halliday's (1994: 302) *tone 2*).

Exclamation marks !   refer to utterances against expectation (for example, surprise, shock, etc.). This corresponds to Halliday's (1994: 303) *tone 5*, rising-falling.

Stressed syllables/loudness

Words in capitals   YES   are used to render particularly emphasized syllables and/or to indicate increasing volume.

Italics	*yes*	indicate that the word or passage in italics was spoken in a considerably lower voice.

Contextual commentaries

Empty brackets	( )	are used to indicate that passages of the interviews could not be transcribed because of technical defects of the recordings or because the applicants spoke too low or in a slurry manner, so that they could not be understood acoustically.
Words in brackets	(yes)	indicate passages of the interviews that were difficult to understand acoustically and could not be rendered with a hundred percent accuracy.

Paralinguistic and non-verbal information

Words in square brackets	[laughs]	render information on relevant non-verbal behaviour.

Fillers

The most frequent fillers are rendered as follows:

umm, mmh		applicant is thinking about it
mhm		consent
oh		exclamation particle that indicates surprise, shock, disappointment etc.

Pauses

Three periods	…	render short pauses (hesitations) within a turn that last no longer than one second.
Square brackets containing information on the number of seconds [2 sec.]		render longer pauses (more than one second).

Other transcription conventions

Hyphen	-	The speaker reformulates her utterance.
Slashes with "Interviewer" in		Interviewer says something. The utterances of the interviewer were usually not rendered

between /Interviewer/	in the transcription as they were not part of the original study the interviews were transcribed for.
Minimal responses in pointed brackets <mhm>	Minimal responses that the interviewee makes with regard to an utterance of the interviewer (without rendering the exact number of minimal responses or their timing).
Words, phrases or sentences in quotation marks (…) and then he said to me: "Why don't you think about it …"	render speech quoted by an applicant.

6. Bibliography

Adelswärd, Viveka. 1988. *Styles of success: On impression management as collaborative action in job interviews*. Unpublished Ph.D. thesis, University of Linköping.

Adolphs, Svenja/Dawn Knight. 2010. "Building a spoken corpus". In: O'Keeffe, Anne/Michael McCarthy (eds.). *The Routledge Handbook of Corpus Linguistics*. London. 38–52.

Adolphs, Svenja/Ronald Carter. 2013. *Spoken corpus linguistics: From monomodal to multimodal*. New York.

Auer, Peter. 1998. "Learning how to play the game: An investigation of role-played job interviews in East Germany". *Text* 18 (1). 7–38.

Bennett, Gena. 2010. *Using Corpora in the language learning classroom: Corpus linguistics for teachers*. Ann Arbor.

Biber, Douglas. 1993. "Representativeness in corpus design". *Literary and Linguistic Computing* 8/4. 243–257.

Biegeleisen, Jacob. ⁴1994. *Make your job interview a success: A guide for the career-minded job seeker*. Upper Saddle River.

Bloomfield, Leonard (ed.). 1917. *Tagalog texts with grammatical analysis* (University of Illinois Studies in Language and Literature 3.2–4). Urbana.

Bogaers, Iris. 1998. "Gender in job interviews: Some implications of verbal interactions of women and men". *International Journal of the Sociology of Language* 129. 35–58.

Collins Cobuild Advanced Dictionary (CCAD). ⁶2009. ed. by Grant Barrett, Catherine Weller. Boston.

Curzan, Anne. 2012. "The electronic life of texts: Insights from corpus linguistics for all fields of English". In: Kytö, Merja (ed.). *English corpus linguistics: Crossing paths*. Amsterdam. 9–21.

Dahlmann, Irina/Svenja Adolphs. 2012. "Spoken corpus analysis: Multimodal approaches to language description". In: Baker, Paul. *Contemporary Corpus Linguistics*. London. 125–139.

Drew, Paul/John Heritage. 1992. "Analyzing talk at work: an introduction". In: Paul Drew/John Heritage (eds.). *Talk at work: Interaction in institutional settings*. Cambridge. 3–65.

Edelsky, Carole. 1981. "Who's got the floor?" *Language in Society* 10. 383–421.

Eggins, Suzanne/Diana Slade (eds.). 1997. *Analysing casual conversation*. Cambridge.

Emons, Rudolf. 1997. "Corpus Linguistics: Some basic problems". *Studia Anglica Posnaniensia* XXXII. 61–68.

Flowerdew, Lynne. 2012. "Corpora in the classroom: An applied linguistic perspective". In: Hyland, Ken/Chau Meng Huat/Michael Handford (eds.). *Corpus applications in Applied Linguistics*. London. 208–224.

Geluykens, Ronald/Katja Pelsmaekers. 1999. "Analysing professional discourse: An introduction". In: Ronald Geluykens/Katja Pelsmaekers (eds.). *Discourse in professional contexts*. München. 3–22.

Halliday, M.A.K. 1994. *An Introduction to Functional Grammar*. London/Melbourne.

Halliday, M.A.K./Ruqaiya Hasan. ⁶1984. *Cohesion in English*. London/New York.

Hoffmann, Sebastian. 2009. "Corpus Linguistics and the Internet – An Overview and three case studies". *Anglistik* 20/1. 23–39.

Hunston, Susan. 2012. "Afterword: The problems of applied linguistics". In: Hyland, Ken/Chau Meng Huat/Michael Handford (eds.). *Corpus applications in Applied Linguistics*. London. 242–247.

Hyland, Ken/Chau Meng Huat/Michael Handford (eds.). 2012. *Corpus applications in Applied Linguistics*. London.

Hyland, Ken/Chau Meng Huat/Michael Handford. 2012. "Introduction". In: Hyland, Ken/Chau Meng Huat/Michael Handford (eds.). *Corpus applications in Applied Linguistics*. London. 3–9.

Komter, Martha. 1987. *Conflict and cooperation in job interviews: A study of talk, tasks, and ideas*. Amsterdam.

Kratochvílová, Iva/Norbert Wolf. 2010. "Statt eines Vorworts: Ansätze zu einer sprachwissenschaftlichen Quellenkunde". In: Kratochvílová,

Iva/Norbert Wolf (eds.). *Kompendium Korpuslinguistik: Eine Bestandsaufnahme aus deutsch-tschechischer Perspektive.* Heidelberg. 9–15.

Kytö, Merja. 2012. "Introduction". In: Kytö, Merja (ed.). *English corpus linguistics: Crossing paths.* Amsterdam. 1–6.

Lahiff, James/John Penrose. ⁵1997. *Business communication: Strategies and skills.* New Jersey.

Leech, Geoffrey. 1991. "The State of the Art in Corpus Linguistics". In: Karin Aijmer/Bengt Altenberg (eds.). *English Corpus Linguistics: Studies in honour of Jan Svartvik.* London/New York. 8–29.

Leech, Geoffrey. 1992. "Corpora and theories of linguistic performance". In: Jan Svartvik. *Directions in Corpus Linguistics: Proceedings of Nobel Symposium, 4–8 August 1991.* Berlin/New York. 105–122.

Lenz, Friedrich. 1989. *Organisationsprinzipien in mündlicher Fachkommunikation.* Frankfurt am Main.

Lew, Robert. 2012. "The Web as corpus versus traditional corpora: Their relative utility for linguists and language learners". In: Baker, Paul. *Contemporary Corpus Linguistics.* London. 289–300.

Mauranen, Anna. 2004. "Spoken corpus for an ordinary learner". In: John Sinclair. *How to use corpora in language teaching.* Amsterdam. 89–105.

McCarthy, Michael/Anne O'Keeffe. 2010. "Historical Perspective: What are corpora and how have they evolved?" In: O'Keeffe, Anne/Michael McCarthy (eds.). *The Routledge Handbook of Corpus Linguistics.* London. 3–13.

McEnery, Tony et al. 2006. *Corpus-based language studies: An advanced resource book.* London.

McEnery, Tony/Andrew Hardie. 2012. *Corpus Linguistics: Method, theory and practice.* Cambridge.

Meyer, Charles F. 2002. *English Corpus Linguistics.* Cambridge.

Meyer, Charles F. 2012. "Textual analysis: From philology to corpus linguistics". In: Kytö, Merja (ed.). *English corpus linguistics: Crossing paths.* Amsterdam. 23–42.

Mindt, Ilka. 2009. "Corpus Linguistics: A discipline on the move". *Anglistik* 20/1. 7–10.

Mindt, Ilka. 2009. "Corpus-based and corpus-driven approaches: An investigation of the verb *do*". *Anglistik* 20/1. 69–88.

O'Keeffe, Anne/Michael McCarthy (eds.). 2010. *The Routledge Handbook of Corpus Linguistics*. London.

Quirk, Randolph/Jan Svartvik (eds.). 1980. *A Corpus of English Conversation*. Lund.

Reppen, Randi. 2012. "English language teaching and corpus linguistics: Lessons from the American National Corpus". In: Baker, Paul. *Contemporary Corpus Linguistics*. London. 204–213.

Sellien, Reinhold/Helmut Sellien. [14]1997. *Gabler Wirtschaftslexikon*. Wiesbaden.

Sinclair, John (ed.). 2004. *How to use corpora in language teaching*. Amsterdam.

Tognini-Bonelli, Elena. 2001. *Corpus Linguistics at work*. Amsterdam.

Tognini-Bonelli, Elena. 2010. "Theoretical overview of the evolution of corpus linguistics". In: O'Keeffe, Anne/Michael McCarthy (eds.). *The Routledge Handbook of Corpus Linguistics*. London. 14–27.

Viana, Vander/Sonia Zyngier/Geoff Barnbrook (eds.). 2011. *Perspectives on Corpus Linguistics*. Amsterdam.

Wawra, Daniela. 2004. *Männer und Frauen im Job Interview: Eine evolutionspsycho-logische Studie zu ihrem Sprachgebrauch im Englischen*. Münster.

7. The transcription of the job interviews

I 1f

Sex: female
Age: 19
Origin: Spokane, Washington State, USA

1. I'm from Spokane Washington ... and I am a German major. [laughs slightly]
2. Umm ... I wanna be a German teacher and ... in order to be a German teacher you have to live in Germany.
3. Umm ... I already have a conversation class ... at the moment ... and ... we do quite well ... and [4 sec.] /Interviewer: o. k./ [laughs slightly] /Interviewer: What kind of conversation class is it?/ it's just an English conversation class. /Interviewer: Here at Passau university?/ yes. /Interviewer: Cool./ but it's - it's just for our own and it's umm just for fun.
4. I'm very outgoing and I'm not really shy about things and ... knowing how it is ... to be corrected from a German ... I correct people ... from - as ...- as an American - as a native English speaker umm ... yeah
5. My strengths ... and my weaknesses are the same thing. I ...- I get to know people ... and ... it seems like we've known each other forever and then my weakness would be that I don't ever wanna lose contact but sometimes I do. [laughs slightly]
6. Umm ... most would be ... getting in touch with other nationalities other ... - I mean I don't know if it's all Germans or if it's other nationalities but I like to get to know many people [3 sec.] and I - I don't really see - at least the fact that four hours that might be a little too long but we'll see.
7. I like to work with others better. [laughs slightly] definitely. ... /Interviewer: Why?/ umm ... it just seems easier to get more opinions than just one.
8. Make jokes ... just start talking about the American system and maybe not how good it is with the politics right now and just because I don't - it doesn't really bother me when people talk about how bad the American system is.

9. I like criticism [laughs] actually. /Interviewer: Why?/ Umm ... cause it makes me know that I'm not ... perfect, I make mistakes. everybody does. and I like to be better instead of worse, just keep going on doing the same thing even though it's not ... right.

10. Umm [3 sec.] I used to teach my German class when I was younger, in high school, umm ... I don't - I don't have a problem with it at all, we do it at school all the time.

11. Yeah ... yeah ... yeah. [laughs]

12. Umm ... you said before on the phone that it wouldn't have to be four hours if that was too much? could we make it like three or two and a half or three? /Interviewer/ yeah ... well it's just that ... you know the subjects ... are ... - I mean in our conversation we have now, sometimes it runs 4 hours, sometimes it runs 5 but normally it's just 2 or 2 and half /Interviewer/ <yeah, mhm> /Interviewer/ when are you gonna find out? [laughs slightly] /Interviewer/ okay /Interviewer/ mhm ... okay. [laughs]

I 2f

Sex: female
Age: 21
Origin: Leeds, GB

1. Okay umm well I am from Leeds in England in - in North to the centre of England and umm ... I'm here in Germany for six months doing umm - studying German and Spanish and I finished the umm school when I was 18 with four A-levels, I went to Sheffield University to do Spanish and German. and I'm in my third year and that means I've got to go abroad with the bottom languages degree I'm doing and umm so I've just been in Spain for six months and now I'm beginning my time here in Germany ... yeah

2. Umm well I - I studied German at school and I wanted to do it for umm my degree as well, so it was compulsory to - to come abroad to Germany ... umm so I chose Passau umm on the basis that - well my uncle is a German teacher and he - he told me that Passau is right the place you should be and I'd originally wanted Heidelberg but umm it ... - there were too many people who wanted to go. I'm glad I've chosen Passau now. [laughs slightly]

3. Umm ... well umm I'm very umm patient umm with people and especially with people who are trying to speak umm cause I'm English - because - I know what it's like when you're trying to speak another language it - it can be quite - quite hard and daunting umm also I've - I've taught - well - I've had - I've worked in schools umm not teaching English but just with - with all sorts of children, I mean the - they not gonna be children but still you get an idea of how to handle teaching situations umm ... yeah and I think I'd be friendly with people as well ... yeah (...) oh sorry it was the other question? /Interviewer/

4. Right okay okay umm well ... I umm - I speak German an - and English so umm that - that would help as well [laughs slightly] and umm ... I've umm ... I don't know! I've ... in - in Spanish but I don't think that would be (relevant) here /Interviewer/ umm no I don't. No I've never taught, just with - just with younger children. but not with ... - no - but I know umm about grammar and - and how things are put together so ... that would be a helpful *thing I think*

5. Okay umm my strengths are ... umm ... patience and understanding umm ... and - and I think friendliness as well. umm weaknesses are [2 sec.] umm [3 sec.] I don't know, it doesn't really relate to the job but just a - a low self-esteem I think really but I don't think that relates to the job [laughs slightly] ... yeah ... okay

6. Umm ... umm teaching ... - teaching students cause I've never really done that before and I quite enjoy it, querying and teaching, so it will give me an idea as to which age group would be good. also umm ... seeing if people improve, I think that would be really satisfying be able to ... umm - to see if that happened. and which aspect interests me least? umm [4 sec.] umm ... I don't ... - none really I - I think it would be very interesting. ... yeah ... I can't think of any ... - I haven't done phonetics before so ... I don't know if that will interest me or not but I'll - I'll find out. ... hopefully.

7. Umm ... well that depends if it's umm ... if it's a big peace of work that's got a lot of (aspects) then with other people because umm ... they can all contribute umm ... but I - I like to work on my own as well just because it's - it's easier to - you don't have to take in other people's umm ... thoughts and rearrange what you've written already I think yeah

8. Yeah ... well I don't think you can necessarily change them because it could be something quite umm [2 sec.] well I don't know - quite a big thing that's affected the mood, so you try to cheer them up, it's not gonna help but you've just got to - maybe just keep ... umm - keep being positive umm about the work and umm not let them put you in a bad mood and let them see that they've affected your mood and umm ... umm be patient with them yeah

9. Crit- ... umm - I think you don't take it too seriously but you - you do think about what they said in case they - you know you can use it to improve what you've done ... umm but you can't take it too seriously cause that could be quite depressing? [laughs slightly] and it could be just cause they've had a bad day yeah but yeah at the same time it could be a valid point that they've made and it could work on and improve your - your job.

10. Yeah I wouldn't probably be very good if I feel (I'm) with a lot of people cause I'm quite shy and - no - I don't have much experience,

but with small groups it wouldn't be a problem I think yeah, I think so yeah

11. Yes yes ... umm would - would it be with groups of people or - or /Interviewer/ mhm /Interviewer/ yeah ... yes yeah I feel comfortable I could handle it yes

12. Umm how many hours a week would it be? /Interviewer/ right ... right okay yes I can't think of any other questions no. Thank you.

I 3f

Sex: female
Age: 23
Origin: Melbourne, Australia

1. Okay ... where I come from is a little bit complicated. I was born in New Zealand and I grew up in Australia and in the Netherlands and I live in Melbourne. I've been studying an arts and law degree in Australia, so for my arts degree I did German language and history and literature and I do Korean and I do French and I do medieval Renaissance history. Then I've almost finished my law degree ... when I go back I've got three months to finish and then next year like other ways, I'll be starting work as a lawyer and I think I'll be doing international law.

2. Well I knew I wanted to study a year of law. overseas. and I did some research and it seemed the best law schools were either for international law in Passau in Germany or in the Netherlands. and I already spoke Dutch and I thought it would be good idea ... to improve my German and the experience of a culture I don't know as much about and then my university has like a Partnerschaft with Passau and I spoke to a lot of people and everyone told me how lovely it was and I hadn't travelled much in the South of Europe so I thought it would be a good idea to base myself here, so I could travel as well.

3. Which qualifications? Well I've worked as a tutor for five years when I was umm at University of (Melbourne), I tutored umm English mostly, sort of everything from teaching people English grammar and spelling to particularly working with English essays, how you go about structuring different kinds of umm - of work in English ... umm explaining difficult concepts to people listen ( ) umm ... that's probably the most relevant qualification I have for tutoring English

4. Which personal? umm ... [laughs] umm well I've been living in Passau already for six months, so I think I umm understand a lot more about Germans and German culture than I used to, so I don't think there will be too much of a culture barrier. Umm also I think I'm pretty friendly, I tend to get on with most people ... and because I've been tutoring for so long I've learned to be patient [laughs] which I think is probably the most important thing and I just think of as many different ways of explaining something as possible.

5. Umm in general? umm that's a (poor) question [laughs slightly] … My weaknesses? Probably my main weakness is I'm a complete perfectionist which means I hate handing in a piece of work though I think I could have done better but [3 sec.] it turns out to be a strength in some ways because I'm very motivated which is probably my main strength umm I'm also a very good communicator, I really like dealing with people, really like teaching people new things, so that's really my main strength that's my motivation and I like dealing with other people.

6. Mhm [3 sec.] what interests me least about the job? [3 sec.] I really can't think of anything that doesn't interest me about it (but) what would interest me the most about it is dealing with people just - and probably also - a lot of Germans seem to be really interested in Australia and Australian culture and I'm sure there will be a lot of opportunities to teach English through talking about my experience, where I come from and what I've done and what happens in my culture and politics and arts and that kind of things that's probably what interests me the most is communicating as much as I can about my culture to Germans and teaching them English at the same time, because most people think of Australians as always at the beach or in the outback or something, so I really like telling Germans [laughs] a little bit about the way it really is.

7. I prefer a situation where I can do both because I really do like to work independently some of the time umm because … like anyone I have my own ideas about how I like some thing to be completed and I like to have … the freedom to do something the way I think it should be done. but I also do like working with other people because … you always learn a lot from working with other people, someone says something that you hadn't thought of and it's boring to be by yourself all the time … always learning from different people is something I enjoy, so preferably an opportunity to do both would be good.

8. How do I deal with it? the situation I've always been in the past is where they pained me and I always feel that [laughs] if they don't wanna be there and they pained me then I talk to them about it, if there's nothing I can do to help them out of their bad mood and they're not learning anything from me being there, then it's a waste of their time and money and a waste of my time, so in that situation usually I'd say … "well maybe we should take a break and meet again tomorrow because you

don't learn anything if you are in a bad mood and if you are not willing to listen to solutions to how you can overcome that bad mood".

9. It probably depends from whom the criticism comes. from close friends and family I tend to be a little bit ... umm touchy about certain kinds of criticism but it's something I've definitely recognized as a problem and work on. but from other people, from employers, from people who aren't personal friends and so on it's really not a problem, I listen to the criticism and think about it as objectively as I can and if I think there's something correct in that piece of criticism then I take it on bi - on board and try to work with it. but if I think that it's ( ) criticism, so it's ... just coming from jealousy or dislike or something else, then I ignore it.

10. Absolutely [laughs] I was public speaking captain at school [laughs] so [laughs] for about five years I was a debating captain as well, so we were always ... speaking in competitions, arguing in public that kind of thing, then at university I was also doing the debating club, then doing law you absolutely have to speak in public, in particular as part of my degree I did a subject called ( ) practice which was a real court subject, so we've groups of people, we took turns to be chief barrister and chief solicitor and we went to the real supreme court in Victoria before real judges and argue real cases, so after that I have no fear of public speaking at all. [laughs]

11. Absolutely I mean [2 sec.] being an Australian student coming to study in Germany the one thing I know I can do is go into a situation that's new and overcome it and (grow up), so I'm confident that whatever comes up, I can deal with it.

12. Umm yes what type of umm hours are we talking about and what times - days of the week? /Interviewer/ umm I'm actually pretty lucky because I tend to have classes either in the morning or the afternoons, I could probably work any and I'm free most of Thursdays and Fridays so that should be okay /Interviewer/ and umm so what kind of students are we looking at? are they all Kuwis[17] or? /Interviewer/ Lehramt umm

---

17 "Kuwi" is the informal name used for students who are enroled in the course of studies "Kulturwirtschaft – International Cultural and Business Studies" at Passau University.

... and so what's the purpose exactly? /Interviewer/ umm ... cause English phonology is horrible and then I guess what you're looking for too is a range of English speakers, so American English, Australian - to get them used to as many different kinds of accents as possible / Interviewer/ umm [laughs] ... that's all the questions I have ... okay / Interviewer/ yes I think I do ... all right, thank you.

I 4f

Sex: female
Age: 20
Origin: Rock Springs, Wyoming, USA

1. [Laughs] okay well I guess the first thing to say would be my name, my Name is 4[18] except for everybody can just call me 4ie, my nickname is 4ie and I prefer 4ie, I am from Rock Springs, Wyoming, Wyoming is almost as large as Germany but it has the least amount of people in Wyo- umm in - like the United States with umm half a million people ... umm but I study in Washington State umm the West coast, not the Washington D. C. in the East umm and originally I was an Art major like I ... make the art ... but now I am a history major [laughs] and umm my minor is German. so just the German language and a little bit of literature that I have to ... - but I have to increase my German language skills first so

2. In Germany? umm ... because I have learned German I wanted to study in Germany and also because Germany is just umm ... it's very - it has a lot - it's like a wealth of - of art history and so [laughs] far more than the United States that's it but ... American art history is not as interesting but definitely - and also my university has a regular exchange with Passau and so that made it nice to be able to slide in and get a place to live and study so ... yeah

3. As a tutor? umm ... last year I lived in the German house at my school as - as a - there is houses - there is houses on campus and umm umm every week we conducted a kind of a conversation hour where we were the leaders and we would kind of help people umm make them feel comfortable speaking umm we were obviously speaking German but - and that was hard enough because we were all English native speakers and I also - I tutored a girl that whole year, she was umm 14 years old, going to a private school tha - that didn't have German, I tutored her in German and I umm ja I - I [laughs] talk with my friends all the time I - I don't really - *I don't really have an actual education or anything like that* ...but ... I think that's all [laughs]

---

18 The number "4" is used here instead of the first name of the applicant.

4. Personal like umm I'm outgoing, I'm not really - I mean I feel comfortable I'm not extremely shy umm by any means umm ... and I'm talkative, I think that in this sort of a situation it's - it's important that people are talking because that's umm ... - I found in - just - here - being here in Germany and speaking German that one of the biggest fears you have is just speaking ... and almost because of you were ( ) or translating and umm your pronunciation is strange and everything like that ... it's just important to be talking and be understood

5. As a person? [laughs] well I'm definitely a better talker than I'm a writer [laughs] well I think one of my weaknesses is procrastination [laughs] but ... umm I don't know I try to - I try to keep on top of everything I think - I think I'm a - I'm a good sister that's one of my strengths [laughs] I just - that's kind of a broad question umm ... I don't know umm anything specific like what part umm - like at university what are my strengths and weaknesses or just in general? /Interviewer/ Yeah ... well I'm enthusiastic about learning that's one of my main things that I like to do - well that's - ... that's what's really nice about being here in Passau because you can take ... any classes you want *whenever you want, that's not as - as easy where I go to school in the United States* ... well umm yeah

6. What's? okay well for me maybe umm ... - definitely I ... umm am interested in just getting to know people and talking to people and I'm - I think I'm a teacher by nature and ... I have grown up with little sisters and so I - I know - it's just something that I've always been a part of. as just even now - ... it even maybe sometimes out of place where I'm not maybe WANTED to help people but I think that I'm always ... yeah just ... energetic and want to help people ... and especially if they want to learn *and if that makes it pretty well - really easy* umm [3 sec.] what aspects [2 sec.] *what is it?* Umm least? I - I can imagine it sounds like a great job, it sounds kind of fun just to meet with people and help them ... and speak better English, I'd love it if they had the same kind of program back where I study (then) people would speak better German but umm ... I don't know I can't think of anything bad, (a couple of hours a week and just umm *hanging out and talking*) ( ) so

7. Umm I definitely suppose it depends on what I'm doing [2 sec.] umm ... there is definitely always benefits to working with others as a - as an

English … umm … kind of … Redewendungen oder what do you call it in English? [laughs slightly] no. umm just in English a saying that goes "two heads are better than one" and … I … - there is … definitely (some positive side) for working alone and … completing something by yourself but … definitely I'm an advocate of communication and working with other people.

8. Well [2 sec.] I just [2 sec.] - I would [laughs] - I guess I would probably do that like I might tell my sisters … either try to figure out what's bothering them … and if it's anything that I can - I can deal with, anything that I can help with - if - if what's bothering them has to do with the material they were working with … then we could probably work with that … if - if it's something in their personal life that's bothering them [laughs] or … if it's something that we couldn't sort through ourselves then … I would just do my - my best to just work through like that day's materials and then [laughs] wish my - my students good luck [laughs] for the future and (*it doesn't solve the problem*) but if it's something that has to do with our stuff *I could show them how to figure it out*

9. I think constructive criticism … now [laughs] is one of the best things that a person can have. I mean umm nobody is perfect and .. that includes me and this would be an opportunity because I - I'm considering being a teacher - a German teacher [laughs] back in the States, maybe then umm teaching English in other foreign countries after I - I graduate with my bachelors and this would be a great experience and constructive criticism would make it that much more … umm worthwhile *I think*.

10. Like umm as far as speaking in front of … - like a lot of people or a classroom of 20 … or 200 people? I'm - I - I think I'm better in smaller groups … I'd only feel more comfortable in smaller groups [laughs] umm … I - I think that if it was necessary I could definitely get up in front of a lot of people especially if I … knew what I was talking about [laughs] umm … I would definitely feel uncomfortable speaking German in front of so many people but … for people who are trying to learn English I'd be willing to speak German because … hearing MY mistakes I think I'd make them feel … better [laughs] about speaking and making their own mistakes because it's part of learning a language so *I don't know*

11. Well as far as I know … - now see you haven't told me some of the - the qualifications yet umm … meeting with - I - I've always like umm - what was it - was it meeting with groups of people? I couldn't - and just helping them with pronunciation and just … greater ease of speaking English? *I definitely think I could do that*

12. Umm [3 sec.] I don't think so … I [laughs] one of the questions I had when I walked in the door was what was - that I couldn't remember your name again - what is it? Daniela? /Interviewer/ okay that was [laughs] so okay, I can't think of any, I have your e-mail address if I can think of any but umm no [3 sec.] okay /Interviewer/ thank you for the job opportunity and the opportunity to … be with people and umm … *hope that it works out*

I 5m

Sex: male
Age: 20
Origin: Birmingham, GB

1. Okay well I come from Birmingham umm and lived there for 18 years until I started university, then I went down to London to study law with German law. so I there completed two years of study in London and this third year is the Austausch - exchange student year umm where I've studied just umm BGB Civil - civil law and then umm when I return to London in September, I'll have one more year until the end of my degree and then if I want to carry on with law, which I'm still convinced I do want to umm then I'll do the LPC which is a Legal Practice Course and then further qualifications to become a lawyer. umm otherwise I'm a musician, I play in the orchestra now in Passau ... umm and since I've come to Passau I've learned the - the viola as well, before I played the violin and umm the opportunity arose umm for me to learn the viola so ... which I think suits me better because I have large hands and yeah just another matter ... umm a professor - a law professor who also plays the viola. and I'd asked him if he knew where I could just borrow a viola from. and he had a spare one. and brought it the next day. so I umm *to carry on with that* umm I also play the piano umm ... but nothing professional. I don't play in any groups. ... umm yes umm ... /interviewer/ is it? [laughs]

2. Umm ... well my - my grandmother is German. ... I don't ... that possibly has something do with it. umm ... I studied German A-level ... and ... yeah not French - (*I didn't need*) French at all. (GCSE) so umm ... obviously that lay out the basis - umm the language basis there and I've been to - visited Germany quite a few times and I've got friends in Germany who I'd visited ... and umm I always enjoyed coming to Germany and I enjoyed learning the German language and ... since that was my language, I thought to do a degree with another language, so German would ... set me in good stead for having an advantage over other applicants for jobs and *such things*

3. As a tutor? Qualifications as an umm ... professional tutor or just characteristics or ? /Interviewer/ umm well since I'm still studying ...

I don't have any professional qualifications yet I've got umm ... like umm ... that English A-level I got an A *if that counts for anything, I think so* umm ... and as far as ... communication goes ... umm which would be of benefit *for the job* ( ) at school I was in the umm ... debating society so I had to give talks ... umm in front of very large audiences sometimes umm ... so that - that helps in communication and I also umm ... - since I study I worked as a voluntary teacher at a life saving club in Birmingham for three years or so and I was teaching ... umm 13–16 year old children life saving, so that was quite challenging, you've got very difficult ideas to ... relate to them and it improves - it definitely improves your communication skills.

4. Umm [3 sec.] I'm quite umm intrigued with umm ... Aussprache *what's it* umm pronunciation. I like to think that I speak good English and I - I don't speak entirely perfect Southern English, Queen's English you say ... umm for example I'd say "b/æ/th"[19] instead of "b/aː/th"[20] ... and - but I find it very interesting the different accents in England and I don't know if that would - would help with - umm - in the lessons would we maybe ... imitate their accents? or just - just keep to standard English probably /Interviewer/ normally ... okay Southern English /Interviewer/ okay well that's what I was thinking yeah [laughs slightly] that's very interesting. umm I don't know whether it's - ... I've studied bits of linguistics as well so I've ideas about language and how it sounds umm ... I think umm ... because of my experience with teaching in the life saving for example I'm quite patient well I'm very patient with other people and umm ... because I know a lot of Germans I know the - the mistakes that they often make I'm used to - used to correcting ... umm ... cause I've already helped - since being here I've helped Germans with their English exams marking essays and stuff and I'm used to hearing all the usual [laughs slightly] mistakes. although Germans speak far better English than we do German for sure. ... yes.

---

19 The phonetic symbol "/æ/" stands for the variant that was used by the applicant for the vowel sound in "bath".
20 The phonetic symbol "/aː/" stands for an alternative variant of the vowel in "bath" that was realized by the applicant.

5. In general? Umm [4 sec.] well should I start with strengths or weaknesses? /Interviewer/ Strengths ... [laughs] okay strengths umm ... umm I'm quite a responsible person. umm ... because of yes life saving and orchestra and also umm ... in the church that I went to in England I conducted the orchestra. it's really a small ensemble but so I had to arrange rehearsals and for the life saving I'd prepare lessons so I'm ... responsible in that sense and I'd like to think that I can be relied - relied upon umm ... I can be motivated if I know I've got a job to do ... I'll do it and I aim to do it well ... and - and if it is - if it's worth doing then - then I've committed to it umm I'll be dedicated to it and of - because of those experiences I've mentioned I've - I have to be dedicated because people are relying on me and otherwise you let them down ... and it reflects badly on yourself (*I mean you see*) ... dedication, responsibility ... and weaknesses [laughs] umm ... sometimes I don't know whether it would be a weakness in - in the sense of this job but umm I can be too thorough. I try to do things perhaps in too much ... depth which means I take a - a bit too long over things. I'm quite methodical. so I spend - on work for example I spend - I can often spend too long on it when it - whether - when it really don't - is not necessary. umm and then the long-term effect is that I don't have time to do other work perhaps that *I've got* ... so it's - that's ... *quite a weakness I would look at ... yes*

6. Umm well I don't know a great deal about the job but umm ... as I said before umm ... I'm interested in ... yeah the pronunciation and - and also helping Germans as I've already done as I said while being in Passau and improving there umm ... pronunciation so you don't have to hear all the mistakes all the time [laughs slightly] and as far as the umm ... - I can't say there's anything that - this is - I don't know enough about the job to notice anything bad about it *I have to say.*

7. Umm [2 sec.] I can certainly work in both - both environments. Umm ... as the life saving teacher that was on my ... - and then sometimes there'd be another person of a similar age who'd wanted to do a bit of teaching and then we'd work together and we'd - we'd probably split up she would do umm ... a bit of the lesson with some of the - some of the students - people and I would do - help with others and as far as working in a team goes for revision for example recently in January

whenever we had our exams we were working in a team … umm so I can - I can communicate very well with people in a team and I can - if I'm on my own I can look after myself and can do it independently as well *no problem.*

8. Yes [laughs] How would I deal with it? [laughs] Well I'm sure as … adults - young adults they would try to hide their bad moods in any case but again patience comes in - so patience with them - so try perhaps not to be too pedantic and to pick up every slightest problem they have cause that is likely to irritate them if they're - if they're not feeling in top form. and so I'd just try to be understanding I guess and umm not too harsh on them ? … yes [laughs] *yes*

9. Umm … I think I - I'd say I handle criticism quite well. my parents [laughs] wouldn't. umm … but I like to think that I can strike the bounds between … being who I am and also wanting to be a better person and for the latter part being one thing to be a better person pretty much has to come down to criticism people saying you could do this differently or … and so I think I'm - I'm quite open-minded … just to what people suggest. I very very rarely get defended in that sense. and if somebody criticizes me I'll take it into account and then if I do disagree … then carry on and if I recognize there's - there's truth in what they say then … listen to them and change whatever they have suggested actually.

10. As I said the umm … debating society, public speaking umm … so basically I had to … umm speak in front of audiences there … umm also with the orchestra at church having to umm … speak to people and get a message across how they should play it or what they're doing wrong and - and also in the life saving situation there would be possibly 15 - 15 people in the class so I would obviously have to speak - speak and communicate with them. that as well.

11. [laughs] Again from what I know if it … umm I - I would think yes I can handle it and I think I'd enjoy it as well.

12. Well it would be interesting to - to know more about the job. would it be with a small group, a large group? /Interviewer/ <okay, right, yeah> and would - and if that were the case that there were two tutors would I be there for - for the full hour or just the half hour? / Interviewer/ <okay, umm, yes> but - but it would be umm … just one,

definitely just me as the English - as the English teacher. there wouldn't be groups of English teachers together in a class it's just /Interviewer/ <yes, okay> and it would be four times a week you said. /Interviewer/ and is that fairly flexible? /Interviewer/ <okay, umm> and just out of interest are there - is this - are these lessons - are they working towards a qualification or is it free time? /Interviewer/ <okay, right, umm, yes> well the thing [3 sec.] the problem is that - that the - the huge majority of teachers - English teachers will be German anyway and they will - they will - their English will be very good but again it's - it's not the same as having a native speaker. /Interviewer/ <yes, that's it, umm> *I just think so* /Interviewer/ okay … umm no nothing else /Interviewer/ sure … thank you … no problem.

I 6f

Sex: female
Age: 21
Origin: Birmingham, Alabama, USA

1. I was born in Mississippi and umm I don't know if you knew this but the accent there is sometimes not very good so [laughs] umm but my father was born in Michigan so umm when I was about two I think we moved to Minnesota and umm there I learned English [laughs] so but I also had my mother so I really don't have a very strong accent either way and umm then we moved back to the South and I have lived there since I was about six and umm yeah we ... school systems in the South weren't always so great so ... but I - we lived in the - in the big cities like Birmingham and umm there the school system is pretty good so I learned ... foreign languages weren't so great [laughs] but umm I started with French and then I just decided German since my last name is X[21] and umm since then umm I go to Uni - to umm University of South Alabama and umm I study international studies with a minor in German ... which is kind of like a ... - it's a special sort of studies where umm you - you really don't have a minor it's all combined and I've been here since September and umm ... I think I have one more year left hopefully of - of college and then I will try for FBI cause my mother works for FBI so ... it's a family thing.

2. I thought it sounded interesting I think that Americans aren't interna- tional en - enough they think that "oh we are the super power and eve- rybody can speak English" and I don't agree with that. umm I think that it's - it's really umm ... embarrassing to know that many Americans just simply can't speak another language a lot of them can't speak English very well [laughs] umm I love America but umm for this reason have I now - I've come here just so I can ... be more well versed in interna- tional things.

3. Well I've umm - I teach English here as a - just a - a conversation class, none of the students get credit for it but I started that umm and I don't get paid for it I just do it because I wanted to. it's been a

---

21 "X" stands for a German family name.

wonderful way to meet the other German students here and to learn about their culture and umm to also help them with their English and most people here umm speak Oxford English which I also had to learn in school because I was in drama so [laughs] it's been funniest for them to hear my accent ... cause I don't hear a lot of umm - of the American accent here and umm ... ja it's I - I've read a lot umm of course since being here, the English, I don't use it as much so but I - I still keep up with the news and umm I try my best to help students umm now since I only have about three and a half more months left, I don't want to speak English that much so umm I only want to speak English in the classes or umm if people come up to me outside the class and wanna speak English with me I'm like ... "I'm sorry I have to learn the language so please" [laughs] but I enjoy helping people with English.

4. I like people ... I love personalities ... I've taken psychology and umm ... I really - I enjoy meeting people and hearing about their experiences and I also enjoy learning about history and I ask them about their families and right now I'm doing a research paper on World War II ... and umm ... the effects it had on the German people and the American involvement in that so for me umm ... it's a good thing umm ... it's really nice for me to talk with the other students and to see first hand, not from the book ... because you know you can't always know from the book how it really was so ... and umm just my interest in doing - in helping people.

5. Oh goodness! ... in general? Well umm ... I guess strengths ... I - I consider myself relatively strong umm and independent, I have my - my values and I stick to them as best as I can umm ... I've - have a wonderful family that raised me (wow) and I like to make them proud and I'm very proud on myself and umm ... my religion and umm I - I think all that together has given me also strength ... just my upbringing and umm ... for that I am proud ... and my accomplishments at school and things like that and ... in the USA I have a 4.0 which is straight As so I don't know if I can keep that up but I'll try my best umm ... weaknesses it - learning doesn't come easy for me. I have - I'm not one of those just ... GIFTED people ... who can know everything or just look at it and just figure it out that's not my style I have to really study

and I have to really work at it so ... I guess I wish I was just quicker umm and [3 sec.] I guess ... sometimes I'm shy ... I've gotten over that over the years but sometimes I think "oh I just don't wanna do that", "I just - no - I just don't wanna do it", einfach so [laughs] and umm but then I think it's that drive to do better umm that my family has installed in me that "no you've gotta go do that", "yeah I know you don't know German, go to Germany [laughs] and do your best", so ... there is a saying umm [3 sec.] "at the end of the day when you know you've done your best then just then let it go and know and be content in that" and yes, *that's how I live by*

6. What interests me most would be ... umm ... meeting the people and umm hearing what they have to say and just interacting with German people. and umm ... I guess the least would be I'm speaking English [laughs] so umm sometimes I get really ... nervous, I start thinking I only have three and a half more months here and I want to learn as much German as I possibly can, so every moment needs to be dedicated to German ... but then again this is also a German experience, this is something that umm can - can help me with the culture, I mean I - I if - I don't know what the - the student plan would be ... but - because I don't really know what the job - all of it entails, but it would also be a learning experience, *not just a language experience*

7. Umm ... it depends on who I'd be working with so [laughs] umm [2 sec.] in my conversation class - I started it but umm the other Americans also come and umm because they enjoy it too, it's been - it's been really amazing, we have a following we really can't stop the class [laughs slightly] because our students just pretty much ( ) us but it - it works well with our personalities which I - I was really concerned there for a while though, because umm the other two Americans didn't get along very well [laughs slightly] so I was like "let's not make this into a debate class or [laughs] a fight class", we couldn't learn there but umm *it would just depend on who it was.*

8. Well ... I know how people can get when they're in a bad mood, because I sometimes as - like everyone umm am in a bad mood, so I don't like to be singled out and some people - it depends - you - that's why I like to get to know my students. not become best friends with them but get to know them more on a personal basis and know that when

they're not - they're not feeling well or they're just not in a good mood … then maybe say "are you okay, if you don't wanna participate today you don't have to, if you wanna speak to me after class then you can", but if they - if someone gets belligerent … because of their bad mood then I would actually I - I would probably just say "you know, maybe you want to just go and come back next class maybe, if you wanna speak with me later" umm I usually give students my e-mail address and my telephone number, if they wanted, they can talk with me about it, cause I'm not just a teacher, I would be a friend.

9. I guess that also depends on my mood but normally I try to … handle it constructively, I really umm … I know that I'm not perfect, although I would like to be and umm … when I'm - when I say something wrong, when I do something incorrect or I - I might hurt someone else, then I want to know and if I just say something stupid, I also want to know [laughs] umm I try to handle it as constructively as possible.

10. Actually yes, I have a lot umm … when I was a senior in High School, I received the lead role in the school play "Our town". I had not wanted that umm that was my first acting experience and I thought "how in the world am I going to pull this off" [laughs] and it was one of the most amazing experiences of my life and after that was when I really realized "if you can do it, go for it" … people … - I enjoy being in front of people. when prepared. and umm I enjoyed acting and I enjoyed having an idea or having known that I had a meaning, I had something to say and I want to say that to people and I want them to understand me because … when I know I have something that's worth while I want them to know and umm then for graduation I have always been at the microphone for something. so … I think the acting and singing and dancing in front of people … KILLS any shyness that [laughs] might come along with that and I'm still shy by nature but … you just grow out of that.

11. [2 sec.] Yes it's four hours a week right? is it more or less? /Interviewer/ okay. … it would … I know I could handle it, would umm - because I've - with the German people, I've often met with them, they don't scare me [laughs] I really like them … and for the most part I hope they like me and I'm always up for a challenge [2 sec.] so

12. Umm yes anything just the - the basics about the class and what it entails /Interviewer/ vegetable [laughs] there was another thing about my conversation class that I really enjoyed umm they would tell me their problems, what they had - the mistakes that they would make at the beginning and I could still hear "valley" and "walley", things like that because - and it gave me hope, not that they made mistakes but to me the Germans they speak so many different languages and they speak them so well and I was thinking … "do you ever make mistakes?" [laughs] "is it ever hard for you?" and learning - knowing that - that they also make mistakes and that I can help them because god knows! they'd help me [laughs] so and yeah I - I - I keep that in mind when I umm correct someone that yes each one mistake I correct at them, there's ten waiting for me [laughs] on the other side … so … umm so it would be little grou - …? and what would the … /Interviewer/ and umm the German tutor would be for …? /Interviewer/ <okay> I understand it's - I've tried to work on my German pronunciation because actually I've got to tell you this, when I was younger I could not say my rs … and I went through about a year's or so speech therapy for my r that's why I don't say r the way that Southern people say it. I say it standard r [laughs] so I understand umm when you don't say - when you speak and it's not correct, some people think it's cute - some people thought it was cute that I couldn't say my rs but to me it's not cute I want to speak correctly so and I - I do hear a lot, it depends some - some Germans they don't have an accent at all but some Germans it - it's the pronunciation really more then actually the way you SAY the word or pronounce each - in - there's a music. and I think once you would get the music then … and I'm still working on getting my music of German [laughs] /Interviewer/ umm … so how many students … would I have in - in groups? you said eight or …? /Interviewer/ okay and umm I think Y[22] told me that there were gonna be only about four people hired …? /Interviewer/ <okay> and umm I understood them - umm do they speak Oxford English or …? /Interviewer/ [laughs] okay yeah that's what was fun for me also learning

---

22 "Y" stands for a name.

Oxford English at school because I'm probably the only American that actually - that umm study here - that actually learned Oxford English [laughs] can't really - I've lost a lot of it but - cause it was just for a stage present but I love it, I love the Oxford English a lot of people here can speak it the Germans a lot better than I could ever [laughs slightly] speak it. ... umm ... and do you know what time - *around what time would it be* ...? /Interviewer/ umm ... okay ... and what sort of things will I need to prepare? will I need to prepare any sort of lesson for the ...? <yeah, okay> and umm ... just one more question. do you know any classes that are really good for people like me who are trying to learn German ... pronunciation or ...? /Interviewer/ probably because ... [laughs slightly] ... yeah I've - I take umm the Deutsch als Fremd-sprache but umm there's really not a - that's more grammar and today I have a class at umm - well and I don't know if it really focuses on pronunciation. I thought maybe I could just meet with my teacher cause as you know there are many dialects in German so [laughs] I feel like I've got about five different pronunciations coming from all over Germany [laughs] and I really just like to learn high standard German and what they - how they pronounce their words because I - I'm hearing some Bayrisch coming out I'm hearing some Schwäbisch and some Frankisch - umm Fränkisch and ... I just - I don't know I just wanna stick with one and learn it really well ... maybe I could ... /Interviewer/ [laughs] ... yes ( ) so ... well I - I'm sure that - that umm the classes that I have ( ) and *I constantly listen to the TV when I'm in my room and doing something else so maybe I could* ... I've been picking up on it but as you know it's - it's difficult [laughs] ... I never imagined how hard learning another language would be ... how long have you learned English? /Interviewer/ that's what my problem is, I've learned German for three years, I had wonderful teachers but there was just too many people in the class (...) so when I got here you can imagine

I 7m

Sex: male
Age: 20
Origin: Liverpool, GB

1. Okay umm I was born in Liverpool, I've lived in Liverpool ... umm for most of my life, then when I was 18, I went to University in London to study law and German law in King's College umm I've lived in London two years, studying there two years of English law, now I'm studying for a year in Passau umm a year of German law here and then I have one more year back in London, then I'm finished with studies ... and umm after that I'll probably ... take the umm equivalent to the Staatsexamen umm and stuff umm and then become either a barrister or a solicitor.

2. Umm because of ... I've always liked German since I studied it first of all at school, then umm my parents' friends moved to Austria to a - a town very close to Vienna so during summer holidays ... I used to go and stay with them a lot so my German improved from that umm I became interested in Austrian and German culture and umm ... lots of umm... I've made lots of friends there, so my German improved a huge amount there ... and then when I was looking in university prospectuses umm I - I saw that King's and quite a few other universities offered umm a law course with a German aspect to it and I thought umm that would be very umm favourable when I'm trying to find a job, if I have an extra qualification on top of the English degree so ... ja so I decided to come to Passau and study here for a year with German law.

3. Umm well ... I speak French, German and English, so I know what it's like to be learning a foreign language, I know umm ... you need a lot of patience, you need to be clear, you need to speak clearly, concisely ... grammatically well, you need to umm ... appreciate that umm a non-native speaker might not umm understand slang or other expressions, so use standard English - standard language umm and also ... I enjoy languages a lot umm I think my knowledge of English is ... pretty good, I have a wide vocabulary umm my English is perfectly grammatically correct, I don't have a regional accent umm ... so hopefully

I'd be quite - quite umm ... prepared quite well ... to - to teach the class.

4. Umm I think I'm quite friendly I hope so anyway [laughs slightly] umm ... I'm quite patient with people, I - I deal well with people umm I - I understand ... umm fellow students' point of view umm I understand how it is to be learning this - this foreign language umm so I think my people skills are pretty good umm and I actually really want to do it. I think it would be very interesting umm from my point of view very helpful for me to - to meet some new German students umm hopefully outside of class making friendships I've the opportunity to improve my German outside of the class so umm it's something I really want to do myself.

5. umm right [laughs] she's always a question in interviews umm ... my strengths umm ... well I - I think my main strength is just umm ... I get on well with people ... I tend to umm meet people and - and take them at - at face value and - and I'm very good to make friends very good to umm - to make German friends as well as any other kind of friends I don't know umm I'm just happy to - to meet people and make friendships from that umm ... my weaknesses umm [3 sec.] *I suppose I should have thought about this ... beforehand ... umm ... umm ... umm ... (this question) is quite conceited so ... I don't know I'm sure I do have weaknesses ... umm* [9 sec.] I suppose maybe [2 sec.] umm ... getting up in the morning is maybe a weakness. I find it quite hard to get out of bed but ... I think - I can't think of anything (*we could still be sitting here) tonight*

6. Umm ... I think I should be able to use - to use a skill that comes completely naturally to me, I being able to speak English and umm to be able to use that to teach and to help other people umm well I think it's - it's quite fascinating ... if I have to correct someone's essay umm I find it umm ... almost a challenge to - when - when someone said something umm for example umm a sentence that doesn't sound quite right umm you can recognize that it doesn't sound right but it's also quite hard umm as a native speaker just to put it EXACTLY into the way you say it yourself so it - it sounds particularly correct to you umm ... the whole aspect of language I find very interesting so I think the - the - the pure language side of it I'd be very interested in ... Umm ... least interested in

... umm well if it involved ... umm ... a lot of - a lot of umm ... sort of boring grammar and - and that kind of thing I wouldn't be particularly interested in it but I mean I could still - I'd still be able to do it umm I might not umm kind of appreciate the whole technical aspect about the grammar but I ...'d still be able to do that.

7. Umm ... I suppose that's a bit of both, I mean I'm ... - it depends on - very much on what I'm doing, if I'm ... if I know that umm I want to sit down for two or three hours write an essay umm ... or - or study for something umm then I'd probably like to go to a library, sit down alone, read a book umm make my own notes or if umm ... if it's something that I - I particularly need help with umm then I can also work quite – well, work in a group. I enjoyed work with other people, finding out umm other people's viewpoint on a certain umm - on the aspect and umm ... working with them as well.

8. Mhm. ... I suppose try to ... umm ... umm tempt them into some kind of enthusiasm trying umm *I don't know* ... trying ... - make it seem more interesting, find out exactly why umm they are not particularly happy with whatever it is that we're doing if they - if they're not happy with - with what - whatever I've prepared or (prepare on) ... umm teaching at that moment then it's - it's up to them, except students are the people there to - to be learning it so umm I'd ... if I got the impression I'd probably say tactfully "don't you want to do this, do you want to do something else, should we move on to something else and do something that you'd find more beneficial".

9. Umm ... I suppose as well ... as ... umm most people, I mean I ... - if it's constructive criticism then I'm usually very glad to have it umm for example if - if I'm making a particular mistake when I'm speaking German if umm ... a German friend tells me this ... and they don't tell me this in - in a bad way ... they maybe just say ... "this is wrong and you should say it like this", then I am always glad to have any kind of constructive criticism.

10. Yeah while I was umm in London at university I used to do umm public speaking, debating and muting which is a kind of umm ... - sort of legal courtroom situation where we test a case and one side has to argue for the case and one side has to argue against - kind of argue in the courtroom and umm a judge sits and umm we have

to convince him of our side so umm I've done that while I was at school umm I was headboy of the school, so I had to do lots of umm speeches on speech day and umm price day and things like that, so I have quite lots of experiences standing up in front of lots of people ... and speaking.

11. Mhm very confident and very good to - to be able to do it.

12. Umm I - I'm just curious cause I didn't speak to you myself on the phone ... what - what does it actually involve will - will it be /Interviewer/ <mhm, right, I see> so it's mainly pronunciation that would be /Interviewer/ <right, mhm, great, okay> umm ... well I could umm - ... I only have six hours of Vorlesungen umm ... we have an Arbeitsgemeinschaft umm at some point in the week but usually umm I have quite a lot of free time so umm another reason why I want to do it is because I do have so much free time and I'm looking for ways to use it more constructively, because we don't have very many classes, so I would be able to do quite a few hours a week, I could imagine. /Interviewer/ umm ... no I think that's covered everything. /Interviewer/ very welcome.

I 8m

Sex:	male
Age:	22
Origin:	London, GB

1. Right. I'm 22. I come from London. and I'm studying at King's College. ... I've been studying there for - ... it's my third year now studying English law with German ... law and in my third year you're required to go abroad to Germany to study the umm German part of your degree. and we have a ... Austausch mit umm ... Passau which means that King's College students always go to Passau ... and then after this year I will go back. to complete the fourth year and final year of my degree and hopefully I will pass and then after having gained the degree it's up to me to decide whether I - I go and pursue a career actually concerned with the legal profession or I go elsewhere.

2. Umm ... I took languages for A-level ... because I always umm ... well I found them ... I suppose easier and more interesting than any other subjects since it's actually a liven subject and spoken and being umm ... moulded by yeah the people themselves umm and then I got to King's college and once I had the opportunity to study in Germany I decided I might well take it, cause I wouldn't have this opportunity ever again

3. Umm [3 sec.] well I suppose in my ... - I took a gap year and then in my gap year I went to France and taught there. for 8 months. ... umm as an - a répétiteur de - d'anglais ... umm assistant. ... it's just an English teacher umm ... for eight year old to 18 year olds [2 sec.] so umm ... I know how to teach basically. [laughs slightly]

4. That might help me with my job? umm [4 sec.] I feel I'm quite easy to get on with and I can understand the umm students umm ... well to be honest, I know they're coming from levels of learning which ... for ... - so therefore I think it's quite easy then to umm ... to umm ... make sure that the lesson actually targets their interests. umm ... well I'm ... - I'm easy going which I think is umm - would be quite important actually when teaching students umm I'm patient ... like I said I can - I can understand umm where they're coming from so - so I think umm it would be quite easy for us to establish a relationship with each other

and then help the umm teaching progress umm [4 sec.] having no real knowledge actually of what the job is going to entail I can't actually answer this question very ... extensively ... so ... pah

5. Umm ... strengths and weaknesses ... umm ... well - well - well to the job you mean? or in general? /Interviewer/ just in general. umm [3 sec.] umm my strengths are that ... umm ... once I've established a goal ... I will pursue that ... and ... using whatever means is necessary to actually get there ... umm ... my weaknesses I suppose that in pursuing that goal it might umm ... - when there's umm ... friendships or ties or whatever umm ... that might put that into question then I suppose that's just a ... - a natural side effect of pursuing one's goals so

6. Umm [3 sec.] well course I - I don't actually KNOW what this job is umm going to entail umm except to the extent that it's teaching students yes? so umm ... I guess ... yes the aspect that attracts me is getting to know some German students ... umm ... I ... who knows? I have several German friends but I'm always [laughs slightly] happy to have more to ... - cause - and even though we might be speaking English in the class time, hopefully if we get on, then we can sit in the outside (out) and talk German and that will improve mine. and ... the downside? I - I don't know ... I don't think there is a downside at the moment. *is there?*

7. Umm [3 sec.] what - what do you mean by that? do you mean umm ... if we - if we have a common goal? or /Interviewer/ just in general? Umm ... I feel ... - sometimes ... if I have to work in a team, I can work in a team but given the choice I would work on my own ... which is why - I mean I want to be a barrister ... which is a very ... single profession umm ... so (*I can attest*) *to the fact* that ... yes I'd rather work alone.

8. Umm [3 sec.] I'd ... - first of all I think that it would be quite ... - I think you'd actually sense that (the instant) you came into the room. umm ... so I'd want to know why ... if it's something to do with me ... then ... we'd have a problem. because obviously - I mean if you don't know how to get on ... so no teaching can be done there umm ... if we established that it is me then ... I'd ask them ... "fine, you ought to fire me ... umm I'm not conducive to teaching" and as we should sit down and talk about this if we couldn't - if they decided "no you're

really bad", I'd have to come and tell you and then I'd say .. - but if it's nothing to do with me then umm we could talk about it and I'd say them "fine ... should we just skip the training for to..." umm - train - "skip the teaching for today and umm we'll fix another hour some other time so we can make up".

9. Umm ... depends on what context is taken. umm ... if you are ... criticizing my dressing so I - I'll kill you. but umm otherwise, if it's my teaching ... since the teaching is umm full of benefit to the student, I would umm value very much ... any feedback and criticism is ... interpreted ... however you want to interpret it and I'd interpret it positively and say "well fair enough hopefully I can adapt now to that".

10. Umm [3 sec.] with regards *to* standing up and talking in front of people umm ... my eight months in France teaching I would regard as experience but at the same time studying languages you are ... - whether or not you're actually standing up in front of people you're always putting yourself umm to a certain extent in positions that umm ... - that are ... umm not embarrassing but because your language is limited you umm ... in a sense experience the same [3 sec.] ... feelings that go through you when you actually have to stand up in front of people "I umm - I'm gonna make a fool of myself", "I'm not gonna get this right" ... there's a sense of learning so umm ... having studied the languages and been in positions where I tried to improve, yes I'd say I have some degree of experience in talking ... publicly.

11. Umm ... from what I know about the job, which is limited, I think I can, yes. but we'll have to see

12. Yes what does the job entail? [laughs slightly] /Interviewer/ <right, mhm, all right, I see> so this was actually - was this instigated by you or by umm the - the students themselves? /Interviewer/ right and ... umm ... I suppose that you set about now asking students "do you want to have help with your pronunciation", yes? or is it obligatory? /Interviewer/ oh! then it's obligatory now? I see. /Interviewer/ <right> is it - but umm - since it - it's actually an important part of their ... education you said? /Interviewer/ <mhm, yes, all right, okay> /Interviewer/ <mhm>.

I 9f

Sex: female
Age: 21
Origin: Cardiff, GB

1. Okay umm I come from (Shropshire) which is on the border between England and Wales ... and I study in Cardiff which is in Wales and I study French and German and last semester I was in Normandy in France and ... umm ... next semester I'll be back in Cardiff for a year ... and I've been in Germany for three months before doing German as well ... [laughs slightly]

2. Umm well I have to study in Germany [laughs] umm it's possible (of course) to spend at least one semester in a German speaking country, well I chose Passau because it's ... - well it's so near ... umm the Czech Republic ... it's ... - it's a bit different to all the other places in Germany I could have gone to ... it's umm ... yeah - it's more traditional. ... Bavaria and *everything there*

3. Umm [2 sec.] how exactly do you mean? [laughs slightly] sorry. /Interviewer/ umm ... okay ... well [laughs slightly] ... umm ... well ... how is [laughs] ... umm ... well ... I quite ... - I enjoy helping people with their languages, already here I've helped a lot of people umm ... with their English work umm in the Einstufungstest *and things* ... umm ... umm well I love to ( ) with things so ... it's umm ... yeah ... - unless I was in Germany umm ... last year ... for three months and ... umm ... also I think I speak ... umm ... - I don't have a strong accent when I speak English which is ... always a good thing when you're ... umm ... helping foreign people to speak English and ... my grammar is quite good - quite good so ... yes [laughs]

4. Umm ... well I'm quite outgoing. I like to talk. [laughs] umm ... yes umm I think that I'm quite approachable ( ) I'm not intimidating in any way umm ... I can ... I'm friendly [laughs] yeah. I'm willing to help. ... willing to ... - to umm ... - yeah to help people improve their - their language skills.

5. Umm in ... - in general? Umm ... I don't quite understand what you mean? ... umm /Interviewer/ umm [3 sec.] okay [3 sec.] umm ok umm ... well [3 sec.] well [laughs] umm ... Weaknesses well I think I probably

talk too much [laughs] umm … but … umm it's [3 sec.] [laughs] … umm … strengths … yeah umm … always willing to [laughs] … - to help people *and just to be there* umm and [4 sec.] *I'm not sure there is any* [laughs]

6. Umm … I'm actually fascinated by my native language. I love it. and … I love the different accents and … different dialects and idioms … and colloquialisms everything like that … and yeah that's why I really … enjoy it [3 sec.] explaining to people why we say something and in which context we say it umm how we say it and why we have to say it like that because … that's the correct way and if we say it this way then it means something a little bit different … umm … yeah I mean … - no I just - I was - really … - I really want to help people *I think* [laughs].

7. Umm … I think it's probably advantages and disadvantages for both … to be honest … umm … independently you could … umm - you could … do as you want … umm but on the other hand if you're with someone else then you got umm … umm … feedback … umm … and on the other hand umm … helping you to come up with something a bit - a little bit interesting - a little bit different … umm cause everyone has - has … umm ideas. … umm umm but … you know just two people together umm just come up with something .. umm a mixture of both is probably better

8. umm [3 sec.] not ignore it but you have to just keep on going … and just [3 sec.] motivate them … umm … umm … to keep talking keep talking and if then people are listening in theory and umm … just … you know umm … just try to … hoax them a little bit to - to ask people questions umm but umm what you want and umm … pick something I'd say "so what do you think about this subject and why do you think that?" … and not ask umm ( ) odd questions of the … - just don't say "oh do you like going out on Saturday night?", you gotta say umm … "where do you like going at a Saturday night? and why".

9. Umm … okay if it's constructive criticism use it wisely … and just build on it … umm if it's [2 sec.] nasty criticism [laughs] then just get on with it and just ignore it but otherwise … if someone said to me umm … "you're really not doing this right" … umm "perhaps you should try to do it this way", then I would try it and if it didn't work then come up with another solution.

10. Umm ... well how I feel about speaking in public? ... if it's in English then it's fine [laughs] ... umm ... yes that's fine umm ... I've dealt umm public speaking debates ... in the past ... umm ... with a - *a youth association at home* and ... umm ... but as I just said, I'm not a particularly shy person ... umm ... ja I - I don't really have a problem with speaking in public ... so long as it is not ( ) yeah it's fine.
11. Umm yes I think so yeah. [laughs]
12. Umm ... yes how many people is it in the class? /Interviewer/ and ... umm ... do they learn American English or British English? /Interviewer/ <mhm, yeah> umm ... how do they ... d- do they ... umm ... is it just conversation classes or do they have umm ... television, so videos and things as well? <mhm, yeah> [laughs] yeah umm ... [laughs] /Interviewer/ thank you very much.

I 10m

Sex: male
Age: 20
Origin: Adrian, Michigan, USA

1. My name is 10²³, I'm from Michigan in umm - around Detroit. I study at Western Michigan University, I'm double majoring in German and music. umm ... I'm doing the exchange program at the University of Passau this year. umm ... and I'm interested in music and ... I've just acquired a new interest in language and I'm trying to learn Spanish now and ... trying to learn German in Bavaria. it's interesting.

2. Because I feel to ... really learn a language. if - if you didn't grow up with the language at home. to really learn a language you - you need to spend time in the country and I wanted to not just learn the German language and learn a little bit about the culture and the people.

3. [3 sec.] Umm the job only - only has to do with pronunciation right? umm well it's because I've studied music and I started when I was ten. playing the trumpet and umm in the music - in ... umm when one is a music major at my university there's - one has to do a lot of listening classes ... and hearing just small small differences in music and stuff like that umm ... my ears are well trained to hear - to hear just very small differences and ... ja.

4. I studied education. ... at my university I've taken education courses umm I teach private music lessons. in the United States I teach private music lessons umm ... my stepmother was a teacher. umm I - I used to tutor people a lot in music and in math in school and stuff like that I have a lot of experience. ... teaching especially one and one basis. and umm ... I - I'm motivated, I enjoy teaching, I enjoy helping others and ... it works out nicely umm ... because I can get along with a lot of people.

5. With - as a person or with teaching or ... /Interviewer/ in general. strengths and weaknesses? ha [laughs slightly] interesting. /Interviewer/ ja okay we'll start with weaknesses. ... umm ... I'm ... - as a person naturally - my natural tendency is that I'm not very patient ... but ...

---

23 The number "10" is used here instead of the first name of the applicant.

because I work on - I've worked on that so much that when I - I think about it I'm actually more patient than other people now, because I've worked on it so hard. so ... it's kind of both there are - ... naturally I'm not very patient but because I work on it now, I always keep it in check. ... umm ... so to speak that I - I end up being in end effect more patient than most people ... umm [4 sec.] I enjoy people. I like conversing with people and I like talking with people and I work well with other people, I work well with groups and umm ... I work well with one and one ... umm weakness. ... some - I don't usually work very well by myself. and doing things that's kind of difficult. ... strengths. I stay task oriented. umm if there's something to be done then I'll get it done and ... I do my very best to stay on that task until it's completed ... and try not to ... wonder off.

6. That's hard to say because I haven't heard very much about the job, I don't know ... umm for example how long it would take, I don't know how many people it would entail umm ... /Interviewer/ I don't ... /Interviewer/ eight people at one time ... umm right, I definitely need more information before I can - I can say what interests me and what doesn't interest me.

7. With others. /Interviewer/ umm ... because let's say there's a project to be umm ... - I like working with others because, let's say one gets writer's block or - or - or suck or ... umm ... needs to look at it in a different way. and the more people that are there the - the more aspects you get on a subject.

8. Well the first thing that you ... - that I feel using my experience is when - if there's suddenly - if the - the - the theme is getting a little long and umm - personally you just take a break. ... cause your mind needs a break, your mind can't work forever, take a break ... umm last year the music lesson was a little bit smaller you know so we get up and - and walk around we get a drink of water and stuff like that umm with older students I would ... maybe say "stand up we'll take a five/ ten minute break". the - the fact is not everyone is built the same. not everyone's brain functions the same. and some people can learn for un-unbelievable amount of amounts of time. ... endlessly. and never need a break and stuff. other people can only read a book for 15 minutes and then have to take an half hour break and then come back. umm

that's - that would completely depend on the people that are there … and … for example if one person's tired and the rest of the group can keep going, then I don't think you can compromise the group for that one person. … on the other hand, if the whole group's tired and you know two people are saying we need to keep going, I - I don't think that's right either. I think you need to do … for - for the - what's best for the whole group.

9. How do I handle what? /Interviewer/ criticism. … umm the other wonderful thing about being a music student is … you have to take private music lessons. and … umm when you're doing music study, people tell you … you're doing things wrong all the time. "no you need to play it this way. no that should sound this way, that's out of tune". umm … and I think I take criticism well. I think I - I listen to every criticism that I get. and I think about it. and … I contemplate it and then … umm … try to listen to what - what's being said.

10. Mhm … I'm very comfortable speaking in public. umm … for heaven! [laughs slightly] going back - sorry! - going back to the music thing umm you know, you play concerts or … if I … play a solo with an orchestra or something like that umm you have to introduce yourself. you have to make a speech, I … conducted a choir and I just have to introduce the - the songs and talk a little bit about what we're gonna sing umm … and I'm really comfortable in - in front of public, I've just - … since I was ten I've been playing concerts … all the time and always in front of people and … I have no problems with that.

11. Well … going back to the umm - I haven't gotten that much information but with what little I know and knowing that it is more of a teaching … slash helping situation, I think I could - I really think I could do it.

12. That's a question! [laughs] of course. so … first of all from … what I understand it is you have received a grant. … from the government or from somebody. to … - to hire native speaking tutors to help German students with - with English Aussprache - with English pronunciation. and umm … you're making - you're doing interviews right now and - just interviewing people and how many people do you need? /Interviewer/ <mhm> mhm … now how is it with room situation,

with time umm … is it - is it only gonna be … for example Monday nights at 7 pm in room 412 or is it - … do I get set the time or … /Interviewer/ <mhm> so and the phonetic ( ) /Interviewer/ <mhm> mhm … umm … and who is the German students? are they in the Grundstudium, in the Hauptstudium, are they … in graduate work or …? /Interviewer/ umm both the students I'm teaching and the - the students with whom I'm working. /Interviewer/ so she's with everyone. /Interviewer/ mhm … and are they all Kuwis[24] or …? /Interviewer/ <mhm> /Interviewer/ now are there course materials for this, are we given course materials? <mhm> … umm … will I have access to a copy machine ? will I be able to make copies? would there be something I'd have to pay for myself or that's something the university will pay for? /Interviewer/ wonderful. umm … well is it just a regular room with an overhead projector and the - the blackboard? /Interviewer/ and it's one hour? … a week? /Interviewer/ <mhm> okay and then if I - you're gonna - if you would do four in a week then it would be 320. /Interviewer/ okay. … so just … umm … eight German students. one German co-tutor. umm who will be transcribing everything, I assume the - the IPA and then myself. so … one - one to four hours a week probably two hours a week. I'll be able to use a copy machine. there'll be an overhead projector and a blackboard. and I will be given course materials. … and the time will be sort of set but … /Interviewer/ not really. mhm … then is this course umm required for the - the German students? /Interviewer/ we don't have a break over Pfingsten? /Interviewer/ umm … over Pfingsten I'm going to - to France with - with a group. I'm playing a tour in France. umm … well … umm so how is it with umm - let's say another one of the English native speaking tutors can't make it that day. umm do we fill in for each other? or would you prefer that class …? /Interviewer/ <mhm> I get a lot of visitors as well. they could help. they could always come into class. they don't speak any German. so that would be perfect for the students. … and from when until when? /Interviewer/ how many weeks at

---

24 "Kuwi" is the informal name used for students who are enroled in the course of studies "Kulturwirtschaft – International Cultural and Business Studies" at Passau University.

all? /Interviewer/ twelve weeks ... okay it's already in the second week of the semester and the last week is Klausurweek I - so just twelve. /Interviewer/ mhm ... so if there were to be a contract it wouldn't be in the contract that ... well ... there has to be twelve classes or there has to be ten classes? /Interviewer/ <mhm> ... okay. /Interviewer/ yeah. /Interviewer/ no problem.

I 11m

Sex: male
Age: 21
Origin: York, GB

1. Okay I'm ... umm umm 11[25]. I come from York in England, it's in the North of England umm ... it's a very nice umm town, old and ... historic. umm ... I study in a place called Sheffield which is umm ... about umm - about an hour away from York. umm ... I study languages. umm ... mainly German and Spanish. ... I've been studying Portuguese but I've umm - I've given that up because umm ... it's ... very difficult [laughs slightly] umm ... so now umm I'm in my third year of studies ... umm ... which is in England - that's the year abroad. so the first semester I spent in - I spent in Uruguay. and now my second semester is here - here in Passau.

2. Umm ... I chose - I chose German as a ... - as a degree ... umm when - when I started university. ... mainly because it was one of my best subjects when umm ... I finished secondary school. ... umm so I had to come to Germany ... in this year because umm it's the year abroad, it's obligatory. ... so umm I - I chose - I chose Passau to come to. ... because I - I know it's in the South. and it's in Bavaria. you know Bavaria is a nice place.

3. okay at the moment ... umm the only thing I have is that I'm a native English speaker. umm ... I - I umm ... in Uruguay I did umm two lessons umm speaking English with ... umm Uruguayan students umm so that gave me a lot of experience. ... which umm I needed because hope - I've hoped to become ... an English teacher when ... I umm - when I graduate.

4. Umm [2 sec.] to be honest [laughs] I'm not really sure ... umm I - I like to help people. umm [3 sec.] umm I - if someone has a problem, I like to be able to help him and umm ... and umm - I always try my best to do so. ... umm ... apart from that [3 sec.] umm [2 sec.] ... I'm not really sure [laughs slightly embarrassed] ... umm [5 sec.] I ... think that I - I can - I am able to umm recognize where certain people have

---

25 The number "11" is used here instead of the first name of the applicant.

difficulties. umm … where their strengths and weaknesses are. umm … and hopefully I'll be able to umm see that. in the future. umm … what I'm trying to do at he moment is gain experience in this kind of thing umm which would help me when I finish - I finish university. umm but at the moment I don't have a lot of experience.

5. Umm I think my weakness … umm … definitely my weaknesses are that umm I sometimes can be umm … somewhat quiet and umm … sometimes a bit shy but umm … I think in time I'll be able to change that. … umm … my strengths [2 sec.] umm … that I [2 sec.] I can … - I can get on with people easily, I have no difficulty in umm … umm [2 sec.] in forging a good relationship with somebody. umm … and also umm … I think people also find that with me - that I'm - that I'm easy to get along with. … umm … I'm not sure well [laughs slightly embarrassed]

6. Umm … what most interests me is umm … that I'll be able to gain experience for the future. umm I definitely need to gain experience in umm … helping other people in teaching umm … teaching English to foreign students. umm [3 sec.] the bit that least interests me [6 sec.] (*I'm already - no)* [laughs slightly embarrassed] - a bit - well also what would interest me is that umm … umm … it would help me with … - perhaps a little with my German. which I know isn't - isn't so good. which is also one of my weaknesses. I don't speak very good German. umm … but what doesn't interest me? … oh! and also another - what would interest me would be … getting some money for it [laughs slightly, apologizing] because I umm … *need that well* … and what would interest me is that [3 sec.] I - *I don't really know anything else.*

7. Umm … with others I would say. … in - in what - what sense? … in teaching or? /Interviewer/ I generally prefer working with other people. /Interviewer: And why?/ umm I think it's [2 sec.] - it's easier it's umm … it's umm … - I find when I work alone sometimes I get … umm tense. … umm with other people it's … - I don't feel that. umm because it's - it's a better atmosphere. and umm … also I find working with other people who are interested in working then it's easier for me to work. if I'm - if I work with other people who are not then [laughs slightly embarrassed] obviously it's not my difficult - but … so I can go either way.

8. Umm [3 sec.] okay umm [6 sec.] the umm ... I had - when I had umm lessons in Uruguay. I gave two - I gave two classes to - one of them was a ... - with a group - to ... teenagers. who - who - it was a group of three students. umm two of them were absolutely not interested in learning [laughs slightly contemptuous] English. umm so ... - I mean I know it's different because they were teenagers so I tried to umm - I tried to [3 sec.] in a way [2 sec.] kind of - not - not becoming friends with them but try to ... sort of ... try to make them think that I'm not some old teacher who just wants to ... make them learn. umm ... and it kind of had an effect. umm [2 sec.] with someone older I wouldn't really know what to do. umm [6 sec.] I guess I would try to ... find out what ... - what was wrong what ... - what they were getting stuck with or if it was a problem ... related to work or not. and umm ... try to help them if ... - if I possibly could.

9. Because well ... - well I love [laughs slightly embarrassed] umm [2 sec.] I umm ... try not to [3 sec.] - I try not to take it too [2 sec.] - too hard. and umm ... I look at the criticism and if it's - if it's fair then umm ... then I'll try to work on that but umm ... if it's not then ... I just ignore it basically.

10. No. ... I'm [laughs slightly embarrassed] umm ... as I said before I'm not really very experienced and umm I am a bit ... quiet and shy and ... that is something I'm definitely gonna have to ... work on in the future. umm ... umm I'm certainly not - but as I was a few years ago. umm ... but umm ... I will try to work on that. I haven't really had an experience of ... speaking in public at all. umm ... it would be ... something new for me. ... umm ... but yeah *I can try anything you want.* [laughs slightly]

11. Umm ... I ... umm would certainly ... hope so. ... I - I'd love to give it a try.

12. Umm [3 sec.] is it - what kind of umm - would it be a ... umm ... formal setting? would it be very ...? /Interviewer/ <mhm> I see small groups. /Interviewer/ <right, mhm> okay [laughs slightly] that's great and umm how long is it how ...? /Interviewer/ <right, okay, that's great> /Interviewer/ no I don't think there's anything else. ... right thank you very much.

I 12f

Sex: female
Age: 20
Origin: Tunbridge Wells, Kent, GB

1. [26]{*Yeah well I come from umm Setfoint Tunbridge Wells in Kent umm it's not very big. umm I went to school there. and I did my A-levels in English, French and German. and ... then I went to university in Sheffield and I spent last term in France in Aix-en-Provence which was lovely. so it's just to improve my French and umm ... in my spare time I like - I love football [laughs slightly] and that's my favourite sport and I like reading umm ... and history and watching TV*} and drinking [laughs] but umm [2 sec.] and in Sheffield umm I worked in the German society as Associate Secretary which was quite good just arranging bar crawls and - but most of my spare time I - I like to spend in the pub with my friends [laughs slightly] or something like that yeah ... I'm not an alcoholic [laughs] ... anyway it's true [laughs slightly].

2. Umm well as German was my first language, I started when I was eleven so ... umm ... and ... I wanted to continue German at university and so it was umm - I had to come here. it was a compulsory part umm ... but I've been to Germany before and I've liked it so yeah I was in Hamburg twice and umm Mönchengladbach yeah yeah ...

3. What qualifications? as in ... why I should be able to do it? Umm ... I can speak English quite well [laughs] umm I've taught English before umm when I was in France I taught ... - she was only twelve so she was young but I taught English then so ... it was harder than I thought it would be this ... - I think it's easier if you actually learn a language properly to then teach it but ... I hope that's given me a bit of experience to ... carry on work teaching English again ... - no - umm I love talking so [laughs] I can just talk and talk and talk so.

4. Umm I'm quite patient umm ... and I think that's quite important and I can - I can get - I get on well with people I try to anyway. umm and I ... umm ... I'm - I like to put hard work into stuff you know I like to

---

26 Due to technical problems there is an overlap between the part of this interview cited in brackets { } and another interview.

do things properly if I have to do them and so I'm quite thorough and … umm … yeah I like working with people so.

5. Strengths … and weaknesses [2 sec.] umm … as I said before I'm patient and I - I try to work hard and I like to prepare stuff umm … and … I work well with other people like I worked in a bank and was part of the team which I enjoyed just working with people and my weaknesses umm … I'm sometimes maybe a bit lazy umm … and … I do get frustrated sometimes if … things … - if they're not … going well and I'm getting frustrated I think but … I'm okay with that and - no - not make it … umm - motivating myself sometimes … umm like if I have a big essay to do I will … tend to leave it to the last minute which I'm trying not to do anymore but … - no - that's probably my main weakness actually … that's *being a bit lazy* [laughs slightly embarrassed].

6. Umm … I think … it's interesting to see how people learn English because obviously I've never done it. so … umm I'm - I've always been quite interested in - in umm what umm Germans find difficult about learning English cause I know what I find difficult about learning German but it's interesting to see where - where they make the mistakes and umm I think … that … ja I'd be interested in seeing that and … umm what I wouldn't like about it? … I don't know umm [2 sec.] I think I - I think I'd enjoy it. I don't think there's anything which I can see now that - that I wouldn't like.

7. Umm I like to have my own … things that I - I'm responsible for but as I said before I like working in a team umm with other people but I also love - prefer to not have to rely on people I prefer to do everything myself [shy laugh] umm but - no - … I think I prefer working independently but within … a team having my own job … maybe.

8. [laughs] umm … uncoop - … oh! … I think I'd just try and well just keep calm and umm … not panic or anything just … - just try and … be friendly and - and make an effort to - to get on with them. but if they were real awkward then I think - no - I think I'd just try to ignore it and then just carry on being friendly and just hope that this bad mood is not - not permanently like that.

9. Umm quite badly [laughs] - no - umm I can if people give me advice and tell me what I'm doing wrong, then I'll take it. I'll listen to it and try and change it but … umm … if I don't think that they're right if

they criticize me for that reason then I don't like that very much but I - I am able to listen to criticism and take it on board.

10. Umm ... I've - well I've given no - as part of my course we always had to give talks and in front of the class in either English or German which ... I always get very nervous about it but it's never as bad as what I think it would be umm ... but - no I'm not scared to stand up and - and - and talk umm ... - no I quite enjoy it. once you get going, it's just beforehand you get a bit nervous but - no I think that I'm quite confident so.

11. Yes [laughs]. Yeah I think - I think I - well could have a good effort yeah a good effort.

12. Umm what - what would the form of the classes be like would it be [2 sec.] /Interviewer/ <mhm right oh yeah! yeah> so that sounds good ... cause when I've been to Germany before they ... - everyone always wanted to speak English to me anyway they were a lot - lot keener to learn English than the English are to learn German so it's ... - yeah I think ... - no I'd be happy to - happy to help [laughs] /Interviewer/ umm no I can't think ... - how many hours a week would it be? /Interviewer/ <right, yes, yeah that sounds fine> how many English people are there in Passau cause I haven't met very many? /Interviewer/ <yeah, no, okay> it was quite a last minute thing to come here /Interviewer/ <yeah, mhm, okay> [laughs] I think that's that. I can't think of anything at the moment /Interviewer/ no thank you thanks a lot.

I 13f

Sex: female
Age: 20
Origin: Dublin, Ireland

1. Okay well I am from ... Ireland. and I - I'm from Dublin - the capital
    city - but I go to university in Limerick. which is in the South-West ...
    of Ireland ... and I am studying European studies ... which is German
    ... Spanish ... Economics and Politics ... it's a four year course but one
    year is abroad. ... umm ... six months of that year is working. ... in
    a Spanish speaking country and then there's six months studying at a
    German university. ... and I'm here until February and then I'm going
    back to study for another year and a half in Limerick. ... and then I'll
    finish my degree and hopefully get a job. [laughs]
2. Well I've been studying German since ... I was twelve. and ... umm
    ... I decided that it would be better for me to come to Germany
    rather than Spain for university ... because I'm stronger in German
    than I do Spanish. ... to go to lectures and understand all ... and
    also I like Germany a lot. [laughs] slightly ... I want to practice my
    German
3. As a tutor. my qualifications? ... well I was ... - when I was work-
    ing. ... as part of my degree I was teaching English ... in - I went to
    Argentina and I was teaching English in umm ... an academy of
    English. ... umm for six months. so hopefully that [laughs] would help
    me to teach English [laughs] yes.
4. Well I feel like I'm very open. and patient. well I was teaching smaller
    children who wouldn't know English at all. so I had to be very patient
    with them and I think I succeeded [laughs] umm ... I just feel I'm very
    open and ... talk - like talking a lot and ( ) basically
5. My strengths? [laughs] my weaknesses? umm ... I might get a bit frus-
    trated sometimes that would be my weakness if I'm looking at the
    clock and I have a lot of time left and if I have nothing on my ... les-
    son plan ... you know to fill the time. I might start getting frustrated
    and my strength is that ... well I feel like I have experience in teaching
    English and ... umm ... I know how to teach and I have confidence
    ... - well when I started teaching originally I didn't - I didn't have any

confidence but now because I've - I did it for six months I feel I have more confidence. that would be a strength. ... that's about it.

6. Well I really enjoy teaching English. ... I really enjoy it. and also I like telling people about the culture and the differences between - you know the different pronunciations because ... people are - sometimes have difficulty understanding ... my accent so you know just explain the differences and ... the least ... I don't know I'd enjoy it. ... so ... there's nothing I'd least like about it just apart from ... maybe running out of ... time umm ... and not having enough time or ... having too much time.

7. I prefer to work with others ... tough support and ... guidance as to what to do just in case I'm not too sure ... of what to do.

8. [laughs] I try to stay calm. [laughs] I try to stay calm. and just ... work ... maybe ... do something nice no - nothing too heavy maybe something from ... - like - I don't know - maybe have something planned beforehand just in case that they're not - being cooperative maybe a song or something I don't know something like that - not too heavy.

9. very well. [laughs] umm no umm ... well I take it. and I take it into ... consideration and see what I can do. ... or maybe the person is ( ) right or maybe he wasn't but ... I'll see and maybe look at it from a distance and see if they're correct in criticizing me or [2 sec.] just take it and ... think about it.

10. in public speaking? umm ... when I was in secondary school we had to do debating ... that's all. umm ... I've - I've done acting. and stuff as well ... umm I wouldn't mind speaking in public ... I might get nervous but once you start it's okay.

11. yes [laughs] very confident yes well I feel like I could yes.

12. no I don't think so. no. [laughs]

I 14m

Sex: male
Age: 20
Origin: Tacoma, Washington State, USA

1. I'm - I come from … Tacoma, Washington, it's a smaller city, it's about forty-five minutes south of Seattle. … umm … a lot of people don't know where Seattle is though you know, it's the biggest city in Washington State. it's the North West part of Washing - umm of the United States. and umm …. it's a nice area, I really like it there. the university of Puget Sound which is where I come from - is in Tacoma. that's where I study. I just study history and … German … there and … umm now I'm in my third year here … and I … [laughs] am here to improve my German [laughs] anyway. but umm yeah I study history and I've taken a number of history classes … at umm UPS … University of Puget Sound [laughs]

2. Cause I'm - I'm a German minor at my home … school and I thought the best way for me to learn the language would be to come over here. and I just … started to get tired of struggling [laughs] in my German classes not being able to understand everything, so I just want to be able to understand it all. so I decided to come over here, plus I wanted to see a lot of Europe since this is my first time … in Europe.

3. As a tutor I think people would probably come to me for umm papers and … maybe speaking … stuff. I think as a history major, I've always worked with writing. … so I - I know quite a bit about writing and … I also know umm … a lot of people do but I also know how it is to struggle with a foreign language. [laughs] so … and [3 sec.] [laughs] so I can understand what *people (are looking for)* … then I'm - I think also that I'm a patient person. as far as … umm … - when people are trying - when people are struggling that's fine, I'm patient, I can help them out.

4. Well umm I said I was patient as … - as I said before. .. but I … - I think … what I said before was … *pretty good* and … I - I don't know, I think I'm a nice person [laughs] so … I won't be too mean to them. [laughs slightly] … because yeah I - I noticed like to go and … umm at my home university in … - and bring my German papers and they're just sitting there, checking everything off, everything is red, changing everything

and I am just wondering "Jesus, you can't even construct a sentence in German" so [laughs slightly]

5. As far as ... in general? /Interview/ umm ... I think my strengths are ... umm ... like more specific? /Interview/ ... in general? ... in general I think umm [2 sec.] I'm a patient person like I have already said numerous times. ... but umm ... as ... - as weaknesses go ... I - I'm so struggling with my German [laughs] but yeah and I know English and German, I know two languages ... a lot of people know more ( ) and umm yeah sometimes I don't know I - [laughs] I look at the ... - I don't know how to call the grammar terms in English ... and that might be a weakness. like some - somebody asked me the other day "what's the past participle of this?" and I said "well well wait, use it in a sentence so that I can help you" cause I [laughs] - I don't know what a past participle is in English and all that, the grammar terms.

6. Umm ... most I think ... is ... this is the chance to kind of help people out and it's not too big of a commitment and two - two hours a week isn't all that much. ... also hopefully to earn just a load of extra money ... to go out. in the town and ( ) and least part is umm ... [laughs slightly] I'm trying to learn German here and then I'll be doing English [laughs] but umm yeah and then the time just it takes not ... - two hours isn't very much but then I just gotta be committed to the ... but that's okay I think.

7. Umm ... I'm fine either way, working independently or with others. umm what I prefer more? it just depends on the situation I think [2 sec.] umm [3 sec.] I'm fine either way. I've done - I've done both. ... I think I like working with others ... more than working independently. /Interviewer/ Why? I - I don't know. I worked independently all this last summer. it was my jobs. and ... I thought - I liked being independent. it's fine but it just got too ... as I was working a lot so I just didn't like it to ... all the time just being by myself kind of doing my own thing I like to ... kind of talk to people.

8. Umm ... I would just try and go slow. maybe trying to explain in German to them [laughs] and then they'd see umm I - I struggle too for the German language ... and ... sometimes it can be frustrating, I know ... when you have a lot of ... - when you think you - you've done something good and then you're coming in for it and have a Prüfung

and you have a lot of mistakes on it can be especially frustrating for ... - for you ... and for a person ... and umm ... others. I would try and reassure them that it's okay, yes umm ... everyone - well everyone learning a language goes through this and they make a lot of mistakes it just takes time to work them out.

9. Umm criticism ... first I umm I listen to and everything and then umm ... I grumble to myself [laughs] and everything and then I - and then I really ... after - when I'm on my way a little bit then I look – re-look at it and then I'll try to make improvements from there. but I really try to improve on ... and I do umm ... when people give me suggestions ... then I try to work on it and see - take into consideration what each person says.

10. In English or in German? /Interviewer/ e - either way. ... I've had to do speeches in a few of my classes and in German class too and umm [laughs] I'm okay with speaking in public. umm in German I get umm more nervous when I have [laughs] to speak in German because then I'm ... - I'm - try - ... try not to make mistakes and I end up making mistakes [laughs] and ... - but I'm - I think I'm okay with speaking in public pretty good pretty confident but not - not super confident but I'm fairly confident with speaking in public.

11. Yeah I think so.

12. Umm ... what exactly would I be ... doing? I mean would I be sitting in an office like this, kind of just one and one with students? or would they schedule appointments? or would I just be like ... have the door open and would they come in? /Interviewer/ <mhm mhm mhm mhm> so it - it is - what I'm doing kind of - like "eine Übung" to one of the classes ... okay? <yeah, mhm> so it sounds pretty interesting to [laughs] I think ... yeah people was asking me "would you wanna be a teacher or something like that" and I would say "I don't know maybe" but I think it would be kind of fun to do something like that [laughs] possibly. umm how much people would it normally be? /Interviewer/ <mhm> yeah so you kind of give me material - you give me the materials on what to go over and then ... from there I just ... /Interviewer/ <yeah, mhm> okay yeah and I - I don't know if you've talked to the other people for ... about this? /Interviewer/ <mhm, yeah> yeah cause I don't know umm ... I know the Germans learn ... British English

... a lot and I - I speak American English. /Interviewer/ <mhm, yeah> yeah I just wanted to make sure [laughs] ... yeah /Interviewer/ umm I'm not sure ... I can't think of any questions right now but that - it sounds pretty - pretty cool kind of to ... - [laughs slightly] but would I kind of go round like ... practice - we practice ... some pronunciation stuff and then would I kind of talk to them ... like ...? /Interviewer/ <yeah> okay and so we'd like read over that and then ... like say "oh you read it, you read it" and then we kind of go round reading and then ... as they read it, they read slowly and I'd say "no ... this is" - how to pronounce the word or something ... [laughs] okay [laughs]

I 15f

Sex: female
Age: 21
Origin: London, GB

1. Okay umm I'm originally from Hong-Kong. but I've been studying in England for about ... nine years. ... and I'm studying law right now ... and I'm in my third year. of studying ... and yeah I'm doing German law only ... in the university of Passau for a year. so

2. Umm I've always been learning German for quite a while and ... I thought ... a year out would be good. to ... know - get to broaden my experience and ... see what university is in other European countries like so yeah

3. Umm ... well I guess ... what do you mean ... by that? /Interviewer/ well ... I've taught English before to umm Chinese kids. mainly concerning speaking as well. ... and umm ... and I've teach - I've taught them grammar before but ... it was mainly to do with speaking, so when they - be- before they go to ... England - so I'll teach them some ... English in Hong-Kong. cause I go back every summer [2 sec.] for my holidays. so ... I guess that would give me advantage for ... teaching pronunciation and things like that ... so

4. Personal qualifications? ... well isn't it the same as the other question? /Interviewer/ oh ... I'm very outgoing. I talk a lot [laughs] well I guess they really need someone to talk to as well. on top of doing exercises and stuff. which is ... - well it's not boring but it's ... very ... rigid. ... and ... I - I'd be free after lessons if they wanna talk to me in English ... so ... I'm pretty easy to get on with ... *right*

5. My strengths? ... right ... umm ... I'm very hard working ... umm [2 sec.] oh [laughs] I don't know *what my strengths actually are* ... I don't know well in terms of ... being advantageous to the job or just ... in general? /Interviewer/ okay shall I start with weaknesses first actually. umm [2 sec.] I - I don't know [2 sec.] weaknesses? ... I guess I'm shy when it comes to speaking German. ... but I guess it shouldn't affect it a lot cause ... this job requires me to speak English. but ... when I meet some German people I tend to speak English to them which is bad cause I'm here for learning German. but apart from that

my strengths ... I work very hard. ... umm ... I get on with people a lot ... usually ... umm ... I'm quite good at languages ... so I'd say cause I can speak ... quite a few fluently. [2 sec.] yeah and I like travelling a lot.

6. Umm ... most and least? umm ... most ... get to meet more people. ... plus ... I know in class I have to speak to them in English ... but if I become friends with them it would be mutual beneficial cause they can help me out with my German as well ... and least would be ... the hours ... that you do. ... I guess it must be pretty tyring to teach. ... when you have to have 100% concentration. cause as a student. you can so wonder off sometimes like in class but if you're the one teaching you have to have hundred percent concentration there ... so yeah

7. With others. I find it ... - cause you can get other people's ideas and - and improve your own ones as well ... when you communicate with other people ... *yeah*

8. How do I deal with it? umm ... I'll try not to get on their nerves even more. cause ... it doesn't help if you yell at them ... cause sometimes [laughs] I get moody in class and it just annoys me more when the teacher ... - I don't know, I just guess I'd try ... to keep it off a bit ... and not to ... like ... wind them up even more ... yeah

9. How do I handle criticism? ... umm if it's valid and worthwhile then ... yeah I would listen to it. and see if I can improve myself.

10. Umm ... well since I'm studying law we sometimes have to make presentations in front of the whole class anyway ... or sometimes you have to ... speak in front of umm ... - like the whole lecture theatre full of about 200 people. and I don't ... really get scared of speaking. ... or I would be [laughs] if it was in German but if it's in English I'd be fine. ... yeah so ... I guess it helps studying law cause you ... have to get into practice ... in terms of public speaking ... *so ... I'm quite fine with that*

11. Yes ... *I think so.*

12. Umm so ... if I do get chosen ... is it just two hours a week? /Interviewer/ two hours a week. ... and umm ... can it be any time or it has to be fixed? /Interviewer/ right yeah *cause my time table is quite a- ... a bit full already* ... I'm just worried that it'll clash. ... and how many students do you work with a time? /Interviewer/ <mhm, right> okay

so it - you basically - say get a piece of ... reading and you get them to read out and you correct /Interviewer/ <mhm, okay> okay ... that's fine. and when will we find out? /Interviewer/ <mhm, okay> november. right. okay

I 16m

Sex: male
Age: 21
Origin: Kent, GB

1. Umm well I'm here in Passau to umm … learn a bit of law … umm
   I come from the umm King's College London. umm I've studied two
   years there already and umm basically following the set course that
   most people take in England. … which is you know you go to university after school and then … - now I'm twenty-one, I'm in my third
   year. and this is the third of four years … and umm then after this
   year I'll do my diploma and go back to England and finish my degree
   in English law. … about myself. I'm half English half German. …
   I've - I've lived in … let's see in England first and in Pakistan … and in
   Saudi-Arabia … well I'm trying not to say Saudi-Arabien and
   Pakistan … cause I'm kind of used to saying it when I'm in Germany.
   … umm I spent four and a half years in Pakistan and I went to an
   American school there. and there are all these ideas about - about you
   know American style of life and baseball and this kind of thing and
   then I finally went to America. … and then in the summer of ninety-
   nine all my dreams were destroyed [laughs] cause … it just wasn't
   as good as it sounds. … umm then I went …- spent nine months in
   England. … in umm virtually in the ( ) … and umm waiting for that
   to end … and then I just umm went back to umm … the middle east
   to Saudia-Arabia and spent two or three years there and was then sent
   off to boarding school. … to - to - to a very posh one. [laughs] in umm
   in Kent. we had to wear … a very nice uniform in there … wearing
   collar and Kravatte … and umm I spent … umm … from the age of
   thirteen till eighteen there. and then I luckily was going to King's College London. my umm [laughs] my results were not what they wanted
   but I was very lucky to get in. which is what I'm happy about. umm
   … what else do you want to know? about brothers and sisters or parents or …? /Interviewer/ well my father is now retired. he umm … was
   working for … umm well it's funny it's called a ventice which is a hex-
   farmer or cell-farmer and umm … my mother … plays bridge and golf
   … and umm my brother is already a umm solicitor in London yes. …

he is umm ten years my senior. ... or nine and a half ... roughly ten years my senior. and my sister ... is seven and half years my senior and she is spending six months right now in Australia. just having a little time off from her life. she's a physiotherapist. ... and umm she's also doing some physiotherapy in Australia with little children. ... and then ... have you heard of the flying doctors? ... yes, she's doing once a week flying yeah ... flying with them to the middle of nowhere ... to umm - to shacks where people live. ... it's umm - I'm quite scared for her because some of the people there isn't ... - in - out in the outback in the big ... - big nowhere there's towns full of - just umm full of the native Australians, the aborigines ... there ... they got many problems with lack of money, lack of jobs, therefore are going to alcoholism and that kind of thing. so ... - so then she is living right next door to a - umm alcohol rehabilitation centre. ... which is ... why I'm a bit worried about her. oh yeah ... and then I received a package from her today ... cause my birthday was three days ago /Interviewer/ thanks. and it was - and it was full of liqueurs. ... yeah cause - cause in Passau compared to ... where my grandmother lives near Dortmund there is ... no liqueurs. and there was all liqueurs in this. so she sent me all this different English kind Dutch kind of liqueurs. which I'm very happy about and I ... - you're putting on weight unfortunately. ... what else do you wanna talk about? /Interviewer/ yeah cause I can talk yeah you know for England really.

2. Umm well I chose - I - well I wanted to really study in Germany. cause my German has never been perfect. umm I've got a big problem with grammar ... having - well I learned my German just from another - from a little words here and a little words there. ... so the mistakes I had have been cemented into ... - into my language. and ... basically yeah ... hopefully but being here ... being immersed in ... - in the German language which I haven't been so far. I've been speaking English of course ... the four weeks I've been here [laughs] I just have to - have to find out the mistakes in my language. umm ... yeah well it's ... we don't have the choice of university so umm Passau is obviously the only university to go to in our course. and umm if I could have I had gone to university in Heidelberg or - or somewhere else. ... umm but being half German that's I think the other reason why I chose to study in Germany.

3. Umm [3 sec.] well I have no qualifications as such. Umm I ... - I'm English. which does help. this job as a tutor is for ... pronunciation. I ... believe I can pronounce most things pretty correctly. ... unless I'm with my friends then I tend to speak a little "wow wow wow wow" that kind of thing. but ... yeah having li - lived in London. - in east London for the last ... year ... I kind of picked up a few ... bits of slang. and you kind of ... slur many words *and that kind of thing* well that's ... gosh! ... it's difficult. ... When I used to speak to my friends and parents ... then you have to be very clear and I think almost stand straight your hands down by your sides and be very polite. ... umm ... in terms of umm ... pronunciation just umm ... a whole ... - umm 21 years now? 21 years of speaking - umm speaking ... - umm 19 years of speaking English. [laughs slightly]

4. Personal qualifications? Umm ... I tend to be pretty friendly. Umm sometimes I mumble. sometimes I get carried away and I don't hear my voice too much. that's why this has taken so long. Umm having spent a lot of time abroad speaking English is not really a problem for me

5. Well strengths. ... I have no weaknesses really. [laughs slightly] Umm ... strengths and weaknesses? umm ... well I'm quite a passionate person. which means that sometimes I get talking and talking and sometimes ... yeah so I can be quite serious ... do the opposite ... sit down and everything in terms of ... I love to be punctual. that's a German thing I think. yes ... cause I can't stand it ... with my girl-friend she likes to hang around a bit and ... well it gets on my nerves. ... you know I tend to be rather ... early sometimes ... that's a benefit of the Akademische Viertel here. umm you turn up and then there's fifteen minutes to wait. that's quite a good idea here. in England you have - everything starts on the hour. ... so you turn up for your lecture and then people are leaving, there's a big commotion - a big traffic. ... that's pretty well ... umm ... I'm friendly ... I got a very bad sense of humour just very simple ... umm ... next question.

6. Umm ... I think ... a ... slight fear I have. ... of standing up ... you know ... to umm [2 sec.] help people - coming to improve and there is a - a somewhat - a pressure on me. I get paid - I get a certain financial remuneration that is involved. and you feel like you're - you ... have

responsibility. it's just like any other job or any other task you have to do … when there's pressure on you … you feel like you have to perform - you have to be … - what's ex - expected from you. ( ) umm … least … I think mostly this is a challenge. … it's the fact of having to - to stand in front of all the people. … and you're being focused on. so that's what … umm I think … it's - it's one answer for both. there's both a positive and a negative side ( )

7. Umm … depends who they are. … umm … cause recently I had to - I had to choose a question for … a seminar in umm … Privatrecht. [2 sec.] I was … - could work on myself, work with this one person or find someone I like. luckily I could do it with 15[27]. yes … but depending on the person. … then … I'm pretty much a leader. … but I - I'm not - if there is - if there are people who like to lead lead lead lead … and they're getting very pushy then … so I can find it a bit threatening. yeah so … in that situation … I'm not - I just keep quiet … and prefer to shut up

8. Get out the cane … and … beat them a little bit. … umm just umm … be friendly and don't push them too much. cause … otherwise they might have some personal problems … or just be hanging about, they're … - they're there to learn. so they should learn a little bit. push them a little bit. … but maybe they'll come back the next day and it will be better then. so … just be friendly, involve them, don't leave them out … don't [2 sec.] single them out either. … they're here to learn. it's for their own benefit. if they really don't learn anything [2 sec.] then umm … there's nothing I can do about it. … there - there's not so much you can do … next question.

9. Umm … fairly badly sometimes. but umm … depends who it is. … umm no one likes to be criticised. [2 sec.] umm I think … I do handle it better than I did … maybe five years ago. I - I take it very personal. … so if someone criticizes me. … I take it personal. but … I don't … really … - sure it - it hurts inside. but it just … pushes me into doing better, to … strive to do well

---

27 "15" stands for the name of the applicant.

10. Umm ... that makes me think of my birthday. I was very drunk. and I was walking through the streets of Passau shouting out loud and singing ... so ... that's a bit of experience with speaking in public. but ... umm ... I'm experienced from ... school, ... from university, speaking in class ... we have to - you have to make it quite ... - bring it across ... in terms of presentations or things like that ... I have five minutes experience you know with role play ... [laughs slightly] ... but if you're thinking of presentations in terms of ... in front of a whole lecture auditorium ... no ... umm [3 sec.] I think as I said before ... it's speaking in front of all these ... eyes looking at you ... that excites me.

11. Umm ... I feel a bit like I do before ... having ... - I did before I had a driving lesson ... or a golf lesson or you know or any kind of lesson. ... you know you're not - ... I'm not quite - I haven't done this before really. so - but I feel confident I can do it because I don't see why I shouldn't be able to do it ... as there is just people who want to hear my voice and yeah it's just people coming here looking for advice and yeah ... speak to them and help ... and I've helped people before. in - in many different situations, so I don't see why ... I shouldn't be able to handle it ... and I - from my experience, German students are here to learn and to - they want to learn ... so I think ... umm this umm ... - this lesson will be mutual beneficial for the students and for myself. ... you know for my CV, my curriculum vitae and umm

12. Umm ... no ... nothing really.

I 17m

Sex: male
Age: 21
Origin: Hull, Yorkshire, GB

1. Okay ... umm ... my name is 17[28]. and I come from ... umm ... quite a
    small city in umm ... east Yorkshire which is a county in - in England.
    umm ... I study at the university of Hull. umm ... and also obviously
    in - being in the centre of the city of Hull. and ... I study law with
    German. and umm ... I've already studied for ... four semesters ... in
    England. ... and umm ... at the moment I am here in Passau just for
    two semesters to ... hopefully improve my German. and umm [2 sec.]
    that's it really umm ... my interests are umm badminton ... and swim-
    ming ... going out and socializing

2. Umm ... it was ... - I've always enjoyed learning German. umm that's
    why - I - I really wanted to study law. so I chose to do German with
    law. umm and ... it - it's just - as part of my degree ... I have to umm
    ... study a year abroad ... in Germany. and ... that's what people do.

3. Which qualifications will help me? ... umm ... I have a GCSE in
    German. which is the school leavers' examination and I also have an
    A-level which is the - the higher ... umm examination in German. ...
    umm ... and I have also studied for two years ... at the university umm
    in Germany. and then apart from that I've spent some time in Germany
    before. I did umm a work experience umm ... placements ... three
    years ago in umm ... a small town called Lemgau. umm near Bielefeld.
    ... and I worked - three days working in a bar .... and then ... a year
    after that I did a second placement at umm ... a local law court for a
    month. ... so. umm ... I'm quite experienced with ... talking German.
    ... although my German isn't brilliant. [laughs]

4. Personal ones? Umm probably [2 sec.] umm ... in fact I'm very easy
    to get on with. and ... - and I - I enjoy ... - I enjoy being around people
    and talking to people.

5. My strengths and weaknesses? [laughs] umm [2 sec.] I just said ... one
    of my strengths ... is ... - is probably being a people's person. ... umm

---

28 The number "17" is used here instead of the first name of the applicant

[2 sec.] my weaknesses [2 sec.] umm it's hard to say really … perhaps … my knowledge of the German language isn't - isn't as good as it could be. … umm … but my - my English isn't - isn't too bad. [laughs] *I would say.*

6. Umm … what interests me most is … meeting new people. umm especially German people. … Umm … I realize the class is probably being taken in English. … umm … there probably might be opportunity to speak German afterwards or … or before or - or out of class. umm that's what interests me the most. umm … least … I can't really see any drawbacks of the job because - I mean two hours a week, it's not really that much of a commitment timewise.

7. Umm … I really don't mind. umm … I can work … independently or with others, it's … - it really … - I think preferably probably independently. … *yes I'm flexible.* /Interviewer/ umm … umm I feel it's - if you're working umm … on your own with a group or … - or with some people … it's probably better if people have one person for them to … ask questions to and … then umm ( ) it's better that way.

8. [laughs] how do I deal with that? umm … if they're in a seriously bad mood and uncooperative … I'd ask them why and … if there's any way I can - I can help solve their problem. umm … otherwise … try and stay polite and umm … keep smiling in fact.

9. Umm … I think criticism is the best way of learning. … it's … if anybody criticizes my German. and … if they didn't I wouldn't improve. I think … - I think criticism is … if you can take it it's brilliant, cause it helps to improve.

10. Umm … yeah. umm … I - I've no problem speaking in public at all. Umm … I've spoken in public many times before. Umm … I went to Japan as a umm - as a representative of England a few years ago and I had to speak publicly to a lot - many thousand people. in English. that wasn't a problem. … and also over the summer holidays I worked in a - a night club. in Hull. … and I had to speak public - publicly all the time … umm make announcements … talk to people that's - it's no problem to me.

11. Yes I believe. … yes I believe I am confident I could handle the job. umm I don't know too much about it as yet but … umm as far as the confidence to speak publicly … and speak English … I - I can do that. [laughs] … I think [laughs]

12. Umm ... not really ... it's two hours a week? Umm ... are the hours ... set in - in a set time a certain day? /Interviewer/ <right, okay, yeah> yeah it's just ... obviously I have got my time table ... to check ... yeah ... apart from that no - no questions [laughs] no problems

I 18m

Sex: male
Age: 20
Origin: London, GB

1. All right then. … about myself … okay … okay my name is 18[29]. I'm
    from England. … umm from London. … to be precise. I've lived all my
    life in London. umm … I'm of Polish origin. … yeah … umm I study
    … law - German law at King's College in London. umm … I'm in my
    third year now, that's my year abroad studying just German law. and
    umm … having a very nice time in Passau … umm … then right now I
    don't know what else to say … what else would you like to know? …
    [laughs] anything else you'd like to hear? … no? okay.

2. Umm … well basically I wasn't too sure what I - what I wanted to
    study before I came to university and umm … my - my best subject
    when I was at school was German anyway … umm … so … this kind
    of - this course gave me the opportunity to spend a year abroad. and
    I - I'm basically here - I really like just to improve my German rather
    than to get any … - I'm not here for the law really … cause for the
    language. umm for the experience as well. it's my first time living
    a - away from home so … it's quite a nice experience for me. okay?
    [laughs] anything else?

3. Umm I - I don't really know [laughs] I knew I was gonna get asked this
    question [laughs] and umm I don't know, I don't have any qualifica-
    tions useful [laughs] for a tutoring job but umm … no paper qualifi-
    cations … but umm … I know I'm quite good with talking to people
    and umm … my English would be quite good as well. [laughs] … for
    this umm [laughs] my pronunciation is quite clear I think. … I'm quite
    easy to understand … I got a good sense of humour as well so I think
    that's quite important umm if you're working in a group. … already -
    like I can tell that my teachers - if they're like - they - if they don't
    have a good sense of humour it's kind of - … so they're more boring
    to listen to. … and the classes tend to drag. … but if they like crack a
    few jokes here and there kind of makes it go a bit quicker and … you

---

29 The number "18" is used here instead of the first name of the applicant.

tend to like - be like more interested in lessons ... they listen more ... they get more involved perhaps ... okay?

4. Oh ... I - I kind of covered that. cause that ... - I'm kind of motivated ... umm ... easy going ... umm willing - umm quite helpful as well. ... if anyone's got a problem as well - willing to help and ... well I got a lot of free time ... so in Passau. [laughs] I really got about eight hours a week here so [laughs] I'm free. [laughs] if anyone wants any extra lessons as well I'll be available. [laughs] anything else? next question please [laughs]

5. Umm right. strengths umm ... umm ... well ... sense of humour ... I'm quite motivated ... umm ... okay it's difficult to - to say about yourself. [laughs] ... umm weaknesses. ... I can be a bit lazy sometimes [laughs] I know that's probably not a good thing to say right now but [laughs] ... umm [2 sec.] I don't know ... I really don't know what - what to say to that question I'm afraid [laughs slightly]

6. Umm well ... most is umm ... I don't - I'm quite br - broke at the moment so it would be nice to get a little bit of money. I'm - I'm not too much concerned about how much the pay is. but I think that's umm .... and yeah it would be quite nice to meet some - some new people umm ... would it be teaching just German students who are learning English? /Interviewer/ yeah cause umm ... like at the moment ... like when we came here to Passau ... umm ... umm I think this was a very good idea, cause they get all the foreign students coming first, so we're here like two or three weeks before the ... umm the year starts for - for all the German students as well so you tend to ... like mix with all the foreign students at first and ... it's like - it's quite easy to just like bump into quite a few English people and then just make quite good friends in the first few weeks and then it's ... - it's quite hard to like you know - make contact with umm ... like native German speakers, so I think that would be - that would be beneficial for me to meet some more German students ... and umm so umm ... I don't know ja ... I don't know ... the group size like - that could be quite big - how many - do you know how many people would be ...? /Interviewer/ not more than twenty /Interviewer/ oh okay then ... well okay then ... nothing that won't bother me too much that'll be okay.

7. Umm well I - I prefer to work independently but I'm quite good umm ... - quite good a team player I guess. ... so umm ... well ... and then ... yeah working together is good. ... so we got projects umm ... for our German law ... yeah we have to do ... - yeah researching together that'll be quite interesting I think. ... but umm ... yeah okay I've nothing else to say [laughs slightly] ... next question?

8. Oh ... well that's quite a hard question actually cause I've never been in - in a situation like that before ... but umm I guess I'm quite good in dealing with people who are ... umm who are not in a good mood. I think my - cause my - cause my personality - I'm quite easy going and ... I'm quite a good judge of characters as well so ... if I - if I sense that someone's like you know having a bad day or whatever, I'll be quite sensitive to that fact and I don't know, I guess I'd do whatever I could to make it ... umm - make that - that they ge- get better ... so I don't know [laughs slightly]

9. Umm well I think I get quite a lot of it so [laughs] I got used to it. I handle it quite well. ... it kind ... - umm but in a positive way ... so if I - no so if I get criticized, I'll try and if it's positive criticism then I'll go and try and ... improve like whatever aspects of myself is being criticized so [2 sec.] ja ... I handle it quite well. ... I'm not - not that I would regress as people say what they like ... then this would really bother me. ... okay? [laughs slightly] anything else?

10. Umm ... I don't really have any umm ... experience in public speaking as such but on the other hand, if you get nervous speaking in front of like a larger audience or anything like that so ... umm if that would be a problem then ... that wouldn't be a problem for me. really. ... cause umm ... *I'm not that kind of person* but ... I think well - I think I speak quite clearly as well. I can get my point across quite clearly. ... and umm ... I think that's it really. ... although I didn't do that much public speaking, I didn't do any to be honest to thee ... but ... that's just cause I've never really had to ... but if I had to, I could do it, no problem.

11. Oh I'm always confident to my own abilities. [laughs] ja I think I could handle this job. as certainly it's not many hours, is it? only two hours a week so ... ja I think I could I'd be okay with that. ... it would be no problem. okay?

12. Umm no - not re - yeah kind of ... about the money ... umm aspect to it. I - I've heard like ... /Interviewer/ yeah a week. /Interviewer/ umm per month ... yeah per month okay yeah okay that sounds fair. - fair to me. [laughs] all right. ... I think that's all. okay?

I 19f

Sex: female
Age: 20
Origin: Bath, GB

1. Okay … well, I live in a tiny little village, in Westfarmers - I live on a farm. between about 40 minutes away from Bath and 30 minutes away from Salisbury. umm, I went to grammar school in Salisbury, so I know the area a lot more than I know others. umm, and now I'm at Cardiff University studying European Union Studies, which is a mixture of French, German and a bit of politics. but I can choose whatever politics modules I want. so (for example) last year I did German, Constitutions and Governance and European Integration.

2. Umm, I had to study in Germany because of studying German. but I chose Passau specifically because … it looks like this - next year I'm going to study in France, in Paris and Passau to me is the opposite of that. it's not a big town, it's quite cosy, quite a romantic place, it just seems so much more attractive than going to a big city.

3. [laughs slightly] Okay, umm I'm quite patient … my sister has learning difficulties and she's a couple of years younger than me, so I've helped her with most of her studies most of her life … umm [3 sec.] that's pretty much about it. I'm quite patient, I listen properly [4 sec.] I don't really know [laughs] /Interviewer/ <umm> /Interviewer/ I think my languages will help me pick up the different sounds. by learning French and German I've learnt so much more about English language and how it should be said. cause when you try and say things like "Kuh" in German, my teacher always taught me how to say it by using English words. … umm professional qualifications? no. because I'm only twenty, I haven't really had much opportunity to do anything like that. [3 sec.] Umm [3 sec.] I can't think of any off the top of my head. I'm quite good at [2 sec.] being responsible … I'd … throughout school, I - I was (fun) captain and I created a ma- do you know what majorettes are? /Interviewer/ it's like - in - it's the Ame - it's the English version of cheerleaders. but in … in America you've got the pompoms, the little skirts and lots of blond, skinny people. in England it's major (athletics) and you perform in carnivals and competitions and things.

when I was 18 I created a troup in my ol - old school ... and taught them and ... that gave me quite a good experience of taking control in ... teaching people.

4. Again I think that my sister would probably be the main reason for helping me there.

5. Oooh [laughs] my strengths I begin with, cause my weaknesses, I think there are quite a few. my strengths [2 sec.] I think I'm quite enthusiastic. I'm quite a happy person. if I wanna do something then I DO it umm... I'm quite responsible ... umm [4 sec.] I don't know, if I do something I like to do it well. ... my WEAKNESSES, I'm not sure they have anything at all to do with teaching English but I can get very [3 sec.] jealous and self-conscious and stupid things like that but nothing really ... - I don't [4 sec.] - no, I don't - I'm not sure I have any weaknesses that [2 sec.] would affect teach - teaching English. [3 sec.] no, I could not (likely think) off the top of my head.

6. Meeting new people. ... I love meeting new people. ... last year I worked in Disneyland and I met SO many people it was great. ... umm ... interesting me least [5 sec.] I don't know [laughs] I'm terrible at that sort of thing. ... *what interests me the least?* [3 sec.] fear that - for example today I taught - I did an English lesson with the Sprachzentrum and I was really worried that they weren't telling me what they wanted to learn and that I wasn't giving them what they wanted ... umm [3 sec.] yeah, I think that's the main thing. not doing it properly enough.

7. It depends. up until about a year ago I was a REALLY independent person, I hated doing class work. but because I went to a grammar school I had to get the train home every day. so my time was set. I had like eight hours at school and then I had to go home, I couldn't see people in the evenings. so it was quite nice to be able to take my work home. do it on my own. and not have to worry about what train I'm gonna get or what time I'm gonna get home or whether I'm gonna see my family or *this sort of thing.* but then I don't know what it was, I think it must have been going to university, completely changed me. I'd - I'd - I still like doing things on my own. cause I like the satisfaction of knowing that I've done it myself. ... but it's so much more ... fun and so much more interesting when you get different opinions of

... different things. *you know*, about projects I do now in groups it's so much more ... interesting and varied than what I would do on my own.

8. I think you just gotta keep working - working through it. I don't - ... at the end of the day if they're in a bad mood is probably for personal reasons and they not gonna really want to talk about it. and if they do want to talk about it they will bring it up. but if not ... just ... show more enthusiasm and try and bring them out of it.

9. [laughs slightly] umm [6 sec.] I don't know. [3 sec.] I think you just have to accept it and listen to what they say and then ... try and improve it from there. I - I think all criticism hurts. but I think as long as you know the - they are telling you it because you need to know it and then you'd move on from it - as long as you take it on board and keep it in mind and try and do something better then ... it's fair enough. at the end of the day you're gonna be criticized for something so

10. umm [2 sec.] speaking in public in England for me is not a problem. speaking in Germany it does kind of intimidate me. the main reason ... being ... that I wear skirts. and in Germany this seems to be quite a big deal, I'd get - lot's of people look at me. but ... actually speaking isn't a problem. standing in front of everyone with them judging me ... does kind of worry me. but I think in the last few weeks I just come to learn that I am what I am, if I wear skirts it's my problem, it's no one else's business and if they don't like that then ... that's that. umm, relevant experience ... I was (fun) captain for my school ... umm so - and I was re- representative, I had to take visitors around the school, show them around, introduce them to teachers and things. so I've done that sort of thing. and then at university, I was ... the students' spokesman for German ... so I've spoken in public meetings about the German department and what we learn ... so I've done a few things like that.

11. I think so [laughs slightly] yes. I - I don't have ... the - I don't have any time commitments. I just have to be in Germany. and I think if - it would be something I would enjoy. I mean if I could meet new people - at the moment I seem to be kind of stuck in a rut. I seem to be only meeting people who I speak English with. so it would be nice to

speak English but with people of other nationalities that I could then perhaps see more of. yeah, I think I could handle it. [laughs slightly]

12. I don't think so. you - I think your e-mail said it was about four hours a week. /Interviewer/ is that on specific days or? /Interviewer/ umm ... other than that then - I don't – what sort of thing would it be - just talking, just speaking? /Interviewer/ excellent ... yeah [laughs slightly] ... sounds fine. [laughs slightly] /Interviewer/ thank you [laughs slightly].

I 20f

Sex: female
Age: 21
Origin: Bettendorf, Iowa, USA

1. Well, I am an - ... not really an exchange student, a foreign student, I would say umm from Augustana College in Rock Island, Illinois, which is right on the Mississippi River, ... and I study German and history... and I ... decided to come to Passau - well I decided to come to Germany. I ended up in Passau because umm ... umm we're a partner university. umm my - my school at home and Passau are. so that's how I ended up here, it's fu - not really the biggest history or German college around, but I've found enough to keep me busy. [laughs slightly] ... umm ... let's see [2 sec.] I - I grew up where I live, umm I go to school about 10 minutes away from where my house is, so ... it's ... not too far away and umm ... and I really, really enjoy studying here in Passau because I've been able to use my German so much more and I think I've improved a lot [laughs slightly] so [laughs slightly] it's - it's been a really good experience for me. /Interviewer: And what studies have you done so far?/ umm, I'm right now trying to complete my Bachelor's degree umm and ... basically I've ... started out with veterinary medicine and decided not to do it anymore and changed and basically just German and history that I have been doing so far, and umm ... just taking a variety of classes trying to finish my degree [laughs], so ... and I'll probably eventually go to graduate school, I want to maybe do library science, be a librarian and umm ... so we'll see how that works out [laughs].

2. Well, [laughs slightly] cause I don't speak any other language than German and English umm ... I took a little bit of Latin, but that doesn't really help [laughs slightly] now anymore umm [2 sec.] I chose to come - well I started umm taking German because my mother is a German teacher ... and ... umm just decided that it would be a good idea to actually come to the country and USE my language skills rather than just sort of theoretically learn about it and read all the literature but not really know how to converse so ... that's why I decided to come here for a year [laughs slightly] rather than half a year ... so

3. WELL I did ... umm, teach a class last term. in the winter semester umm it was an - actually an essay writing class, but we did meet once a week and have a conversation time and I - I do think, that that helped me out quite a bit. umm I have taught umm just on a one-and-one level back at Augustana and ... I've enjoyed it. I really do enjoy teaching, so [laughs slightly] hopefully that ... like ... gives me a little ... qualification, but [laughs slightly]

4. Personal qualifications. well ... I think I'm a friendly person. umm ... and I think that ... if I don't know an answer, to a question, I will ... make the effort to go and look it up, I just won't ... *you know*, give up on the question but umm ... my students last term were *in* [laughs] - quite - quite *on the* receiving end of that. I'd always send them e-mails and "oh here is the answer to the question you posed in class that I didn't know right off the top of my head". so I'm ... VERY determined [laughs slightly] and I will not ... give up [laughs slightly] if I [laughs slightly] can't find an answer then ... I don't know what I do [laughs slightly], I probably ... go to find somebody who's a linguist and [laughs slightly] get an answer, but umm - so I - and I think I'm approachable, so [laughs slightly] ... yeah.

5. Strengths and my weaknesses, umm ... on a personal level? umm /Interviewer/ [3 sec.] umm, well [2 sec.] I think my strengths would be ... what I just mentioned, umm and also [2 sec.] I think that [2 sec.] well, ... my weaknesses, umm ... I [4 sec.] I'm sometimes late, but I don't know, not THAT late ... umm ... I think ... I guess from a linguistic standpoint I'm not sure if you're looking for someone who speaks British English or American English. and if you're looking for someone who speaks British English, my American accent may – will be a weakness umm because I know it's quite American. Umm [2 sec.] but my strengths would be, gosh, my American English is REALLY great [laughs], so ... umm possibly another weakness is umm sometimes I don't listen to myself and I don't hear how much slang I actually use, so [laughs] but maybe I could work on that a little [laughs], so

6. Well, I ... I always love to meet people, so umm meeting students ... of any age or any level I – I'm really all about that, that's basically why I like to be here and why I taught the class last term and why I'm interested now. umm, I'm also interested in the money aspect, but umm

that's [2 sec.] you know, it's ... - if I weren't getting paid for it, I would do it anyway, so it's not really I guess the least important thing, but ... umm ... umm I think that [3 sec.] I think - I'm really interested in language, so – and the English language does interested me quite a bit and I - I love how you can find roots of words in other languages and I - I never really started noticing that until I came here and I thought "well, what could that word mean?" well, what sort of means this in English and dadada, so ... it's, it's just sort of a point of interest for me, just the people aspect and the language aspect, so that's, that's why I would be interested in this job. [laughs slightly]

7. It depends on what I'm doing. umm ... if I'm ... - sometimes I'm a bit of a control freak and – which could possibly be a weakness [laughs] and in that case I really need to control every aspect of a project umm ... BUT, if I'm with a group and I know that everyone is working for the same thing and has the same sort of ambition that I do – if I wanna do well, I wanna make sure that everyone else in my group also wants to do well, then I am 100% for working in a group. if I'm in a group were I'm stuck with people who just REALLY don't care then I get annoyed, but umm ... I think if the circumstances are right, I'm very, very aah... much group person.

8. In a bad mood ... WELL ... umm ... if we're doing some sort of project ... where we can just sort of ... move away from the project for a while and work on something else, or do something else, then I think that would be much better, or just sit down and talk and just sort of ... find out what's wrong and try to fix it. umm, I ... I don't think I've been in too many situations where the students are in a BAD mood, sometimes in a sort of not terribly interested mood in which case I just sort of let them take over for a while and let them talk and I'll just sort of sit in the backseat, be a backseat talker and sort of throw in comments or ... where they're necessary, but ... umm ... I haven't really had to deal with that situation a lot, but I think if I had to, that's what I would do.

9. Criticism! well, if it's constructive, I'm all about it and if it's true I mean ... I'll know if - if it's something I need to work on ... umm [2 sec.] if it's just not helpful criticism then ... I tend to get defensive, but umm ... I'm - I'm very acceptive – I'm very accepting of criticism

when it's called for. Umm ... and I'm – and I did ask my students at the end of the class that I taught last term: "What can I do better? What - what ... did you like about me?" So ... I'll know cause I'm also teaching another class this term umm ... and it's good for me to know that cause I don't wanna waste their time if they're - if they're paying for it, I don't want to umm repeat my mistakes and umm I don't think it's worthwhile for them, it's not worthwhile for me if I don't know what those mistakes are, so ... that's why I'm all for criticism. [laughs]

10. Well, umm I've done it a few times ... mostly with school. umm [3 sec.] I tend to work better on a smaller level, but ... I could ... speak in public, I haven't done it a long time ... I have ... I have done a few, ... umm just sort of random television interviews, but umm [3 sec.] I - I have sort of the same uncomfortableness with it as most people do I think, but I can deal with it if it comes up.

11. I think so. umm [2 sec.] since you didn't mention that, I'll have at least some guidance from you umm as what to do – if I were just starting this job: "teach these Germans linguistics" then I probably wouldn't have even applied. umm ... but since umm I will know what I'm doing at least most of the time I hope [laughs] and umm I will have at least some idea how to keep going, then I think I ... will be a very confident teacher.

12. Yes, umm these students, are they university students here, or? /Interviewer/ <okay> /Interviewer/ <okay, so the younger> /Interviewer/ <yes, [laughs] yes> /Interviewer/ yes, umm it was kind of strange, last term when I was teaching all my students were older than I was. And "Hello, I'm your English teacher" [laughs slightly] umm ... also, how big are the classes? /Interviewer/ <okay> /Interviewer/ <mhm> /Interviewer/ ah, okay and are they paying for the classes, or? /Interviewer/ ah, okay. okay. I was just curious. Umm, also [2sec.] *I was going to ask one more thing, what was it?* umm ... oh, it's four hours a week you said? /Interviewer/ okay. I can do that if ... and we - do the tutors set the hours, or? /Interviewer/ okay, that would be perfect ... excellent. and, yeah, I think that's all I had to ask. /Interviewer/ thank you.

I 21f

Sex: female
Age: 22
Origin: London, Essex; grew up in Brentwood, GB

1. Okay, umm, I come from England ... I study at King's College in
London ... umm, I'm currently in my sixth semester, so umm, I've
done two years of law already in England, English law, and now I'm
doing one year of German law ... and I'll be returning in September
for my final year of law in England. So, umm [2 sec.] I suppose I tell
you ( ) umm, okay, in the first year at Kings I studied umm criminal
law, contract law [3 sec.] umm [2 sec.] constitution law, public law ...
and ... *what haven't I mentioned* [2 sec.] European law ... and I also
did some ... German constitutional law there ... and in my second
year ... I did some umm German civil law ... and then I had again four
English umm law topics I did umm trusts and property, and human
rights law and [2 sec.] umm employment law [laughs]. Umm, currently,
I'm in Passau, I'm doing Staatsrecht ... and also I've just taken ...
umm Völkerrecht ... and ... umm Römische Rechtsgeschichte [laughs]
and I'm also studying umm Italian ... yeah, and that's about it. for my
studies [laughs].

2. Umm ... well, originally I've - I mean the reason I decided to do
German why I did German at school, at school I used to do French and
German ... and, since I was ... aged twelve I've been doing a German
exchange with a - another girl in Germany. and so we've become quite
good friends and so when I had to decide for my A-levels I wanted to
continue doing German so I could continue seeing her. and then, when
it came to do my degree, I kind of had a lot of different ideas. ... I
always enjoyed languages so I wanted to do something with that. but
... equally, I - I already had a passion to do with law. so I thought if
I did law with the German law that way I could combine the two. ...
and so I (ended in) Passau because that was just the programme that
I was on with my university they have an ex- exchange scheme in Passau, so ... yeah, I didn't choose the city but ... I like it here. [laughs]

3. Which qualifications. okay, umm, well, I really like teaching, umm ...
yeah, I already umm, help out some other people ... in Passau, umm,

Kuwis[30] particularly with umm the essays and helping them translate into English ... umm, in the past, I've taught German at school to umm, students younger than myself so helping out and then I was a class assistant ... umm, yeah, I kind of ... enjoy that kind of thing. ... but I thought it quite rewarding for myself as well because ... a lot of the time - I mean, in Germany, people are always helping me with my German, and so it's kind of nice to help other people as well, and also to see what they're doing in their - their life. [laughs slightly]

4. Personal qualifications? umm, do you mean, umm, characteristics or something [2 sec.]. Okay, umm, I'm quite confident, and ... umm ... I think I'm ... quite, umm ... easy-going, I can get along with people ... umm, yeah ... I think I'll be actually able to make somebody feel comfortable I think, because ... I know the position they're in, because I've al - already have to go - have [laughs slightly] - I've already had to go through quite a lot of experiences in Germany ... trying to learn obviously German, so ... I think it's quite easy to see ... where peoples' difficulties lie ... *or the other way round, so ... yeah* [laughs slightly]

5. [Laughs] Umm ... okay ... strengths and weaknesses ... yeah, I get - my strengths, I'm - I'm quite, umm ... a perfectionist, so ... umm ... yeah, that should hopefully benefit in some ways ... umm [4 sec.] like I said, I'm quite confident and ... umm, yeah, I'm quite organised, so ... hopefully *you know* ... the work will be apt to fit into my timetable ... yeah ... and ... weaknesses umm [laughs] umm [4 sec.] *weaknesses is always more difficult* [laughs] umm [5 sec.] umm [5 sec.] *yeah*, I mean, perhaps some people find me ... overpowering cause I'm quite confident [laughs] that could be ... a disadvantage. so hopefully I won't ... scare away my umm duties, but [laughs], yeah, I mean, I've had experience with people in the past, umm different kinds of people, so umm last year at King's College, I was ... involved in a mentoring scheme with younger people and had to go and talk to them each week about their future and their academic plans and everything and that was

---

30 "Kuwi" is the informal name used for students who are enroled in the course of studies "Kulturwirtschaft – International Cultural and Business Studies" at the University of Passau.

quite difficult because ... with the younger children especially, they were about yeah, 15 years old and ... not to ... scare them, and try to ... find their level because ... you know if it's - people from different backgrounds and things, but ... yeah, hopefully *it won't be - it won't be a problem.* [laughs]

6. Umm ... most umm I quite like to ... get to meet some new people, umm I think that now I'm here for a while in - in Germany ... I kind of - I have a fixed group of friends and just only occasionally you get to meet some new people again so it's quite nice to get to meet new people. particularly people who are interested in languages and the English language because that's umm where I'm from. Umm, yeah, I also, like I said before, find it quite rewarding to spend part-time (with) people doing these things and you also learn a lot about other people ... by doing it as well as about yourself, so ... *yeah* [2 sec.] *umm something that I don't like* [laughs slightly] of course it's time-consuming, so that's perhaps a downside, because I have also my studies to do, but yeah ... it's not so bad [laughs]

7. Umm, I think in the past, I've tended to work more independently, well, with my studies, you know just go to the library and reading everything, but ... umm [2 sec.] yeah, I think I mean if it's a group project it's always obviously better to work with others, but I noticed recently in my studies that I tend to work with other people ... umm, beginning last year of my exams, I was always working with a small group of people with our revision and everything and I thought it's - it - it works much better if you work in a group and discuss things and things become a bit more real, because if you're just reading from a textbook all the time then things become a bit sterile ... yeah. [laughs slightly]

8. Umm ... [laughs slightly] normally [laughs slightly] I try to make jokes which, umm, perhaps not everyone finds funny, but umm yeah, I - I'm quite a light-hearted person, so I normally don't (mind) making myself look silly by making silly jokes but [laughs] it tends to work. Yeah, but also, you know, if they're in a bad mood, then try to do something like [2 sec.] - umm which they want to do, you know. ask them what they would like to do (to stay) rather then forcing them to do some ... grammar or something which they don't want to do [laughs slightly] yeah.

9. Umm, criticism. ... yeah, I try to [2 sec.] - to take it on board, no one's perfect, you know ... of course it's difficult if you've ... umm [2 sec.] been working hard on something and somebody criticises your work, but ... at the end of the day, you - you learn from it, so ... yeah, I think ... I handle it. ... *(if it should be okay)* [laughs]

10. Umm, public speaking [2 sec.] *I'm trying to think of anything recent* [laughs] umm [5 sec.] umm [4 sec.] well, something which I'm supposed to be doing shortly, but I haven't done yet is [laughs], I'm meant to be holding a - a speech on English law for umm ELSA umm ... the European law student association. a thing I've already done ... umm [3 sec.] umm [2 sec.] I mean last year, I was involved in umm ... an interviewing umm competition at King's College where I had to ... umm ... - basically, I was ... just volunteering to take part - to be an interviewee, cause there - there was a competition where different umm law students ... umm, were trying to - to *you know* act as lawyers, and they had to interview their clients so I was just volunteering to help out as - as one of the umm clients, so ... that was public speaking, I guess. but also ... yeah, at - at school and things I - umm ... *I was* taking part in ... stage performances and things like that ... yeah. but I think I'm quite comfortable with public speaking, *I mean*, I want to become ... a lawyer, so [laughs] yeah, umm, *it shouldn't be too ... bad really* [laughs slightly]

11. Yeah, yeah, I don't really see it as something scary, I just see it as something fun to do, and yeah, yeah I think it should be good [laughs slightly].

12. Umm, I only have questions as to when the hours will be and everything, if you can choose the hours or /Interviewer/ <okay> /Interviewer/ okay yeah yeah ... I was hoping perhaps, yeah I mean some days I have time during the daytime, but ... perhaps other days, in the evening it's better *with my timetable and everything* /Interviewer/ okay ... and ... so all - the stu - they're all from the student body, the people /Interviewer/ <okay> /Interviewer/ okay ... and is it mostly umm ... Kuwis[31],

---

31 "Kuwi" is the informal name used for students who are enroled in the course of studies "Kulturwirtschaft – International Cultural and Business Studies" at Passau University.

or is it also … others /Interviewer/ <okay, [laughs], yeah, mhm, [laughs slightly]> they're probably all too good already [laughs] /Interviewer/ oh yeah, I think I have … no other questions [laughs]. /Interviewer/ no problem.

I 22m

Sex: male
Age: 22
Origin: Southampton, Hampshire, GB

1. Right. okay … so I was originally born in Essex umm in 1982. then moved to Southampton with my family in about 1990. I did GCSEs and I took three A-levels umm aged 18. (they were) in French, law and computing. I then took a gap year between college and university which I spent working in Lanzarote and Fuerteventura in the Canary Islands which was fantastic. … so I spent a year there and learned Spanish umm just speaking with the hotel people, the waiters, barmen in the hotel what have you. umm I then started at Bangor University the following year. right now I'm studying French, Spanish and German. all at major level. umm … in my third year of university I spent the second semester of the second year in France, in Toulouse to perfect my French. last semester I was in Alicante. Spain. and I've just arrived here in Passau. just a month ago or so.

2. In Germany it's a compulsory part of my degree course. I'm coming from Bangor University, we've got certain links. … because of the degree I'm actually doing, the triple language degree, I had to go somewhere that's also taught French and Spanish so I wouldn't lose my … sort of level in those. umm, I chose Passau particularly … because it's very similar to Bangor in a way. it's very small. there's only about eight, nine thousand students. … and after Toulouse and Alicante I thought I might want something a bit smaller. that has not quite so many students. … umm, also because of the location, sort of right next to Austria. umm, I've got lots of friends currently teaching in Austria. studying. so it's very close so I could meet them … umm, also close to the Czech Republic. already done Prague a few weeks ago. So, simply Passau because of the size, the location … what have you.

3. Umm, giving the English lessons you mean. umm … firstly, I suppose the fact that I'm interested in languages. and I'm doing the triple degree. … so I'm obviously interested in them. and both in Spain and in France I was - it - it wasn't tutoring as such. it was an intercambio system … so I had a - a Spanish or a French … sort of native speaker as

a partner. ... and we'd do an hour or so each week in French or Spanish and an hour in English ... and I had sort of grammar questions and pronunciation problems, that we'd sort of work around ... and - ...

4. Personal qualifications? [laughs] umm I suppose, very easy-going, very laid-back, umm ... my German I know is not very good at all so I really don't mind if other people make mistakes. ... umm, again my - the partner I had in Alicante ... her English wasn't very good at all, it was very sort of ... stuttery, it was looking for the words just wasn't a problem. ... (*it was*) - I know exactly what it's like with German. [laughs]

5. In respect to [4 sec]? /Interviewer/ okay. ... umm ... strength would definitely be the language ability. ... umm, it's always been ... a very sort of strength. - good - very good strength of mine. ... umm [3 sec.] listener. ... again laid-back and easy-going. ... umm... weaknesses? [2 sec.] I suppose probably a bit impatient at times. [laughs] if I was totally honest. ... totally depends, but normally ... very easy-going.

6. Doing teaching which was actually always something I've had an interest in. since when I was at college and we had the ... - the ... - the native speakers (in to actually) take us for the conversation classes. it was always something I was interested in doing. ... umm ... because of again, cause of my degree, I can't actually ... go - couldn't actually go abroad as an assistant cause I've got to spend one semester in each country. but just, umm, I've got the obvious interest in languages and just helping others, teaching. also, teaching is possibly something I've thought about doing in the future. ... so ... I thought it might be a good insight as to maybe how it works, to see if it's really maybe what I want to do.

7. In ... a team. ... pfff, I'm really not (fast) either way. I work well in small teams. ... umm, have done in - that's what I was doing in the Canaries. I was in a team with three or four people. but I'm also quite happy sort of on my own, working.

8. [Laughs] umm [4 sec.] I suppose it would depend on the exercise, on the students. ... umm [2 sec.] just carry on, see how it goes, and umm ... if necessary, maybe just speak to them afterwards or something. just [3 sec.] maybe just a bad day in which case just ignore it. forget it.

9. Umm [2 sec.], if it's constructive ... not a problem. if it's [2 sec.] - how do I put this? ... if it's very sort of ... critical. very blunt. very (cut). I'm not overkeen. but if it's constructive. in a nice way. ... fine.

10. Again ... umm what I was doing in the Canaries. I was doing the hotel entertainment. so I was organising groups of people, up to - I was speaking in front of maybe two, three hundred people. in umm the discos and running the game-shows every night. ... umm, I've also been performing magic. for about ten, twelve years now. so ... I'm quite happy doing that.

11. I would think so. Again, I'd like more information and have a look at maybe what ... is actually required and see the sources and ... how many hours a week etc., etc.

12. Yeah. what kind of material is it? is it, umm, ... actually lecturing or is it just listening and ... correcting errors. ... and what kind of groups would we be working with. would that be the sixty students we see in normal lectures? /Interviewer/ or be groups of five or ten people? /Interviewer/ <mhm, [laughs slightly], mhm, right, okay, [laughs], okay> just to point out the differences between that pronunciation and those words /Interviewer/ <[laughs], sure, okay, mhm> hear the errors, yeah [laughs] /Interviewer/ <mhm, okay, [laughs]> not necessarily the grammar or anything /Interviewer/ <yeah, okay, that's right, mhm, sure> so bringing articles, read through, that kind of exercise in groups. ... okay. yeah that - that's what we've been doing in Bangor as well (actually) in the conversation classes. very sort of similar thing. and how many hours a week are you looking for? /Interviewer/ four hours. umm ... are the cla - I was gonna be flexible? or ... they were /Interviewer/ right. /Interviewer/ same material, so just once a week ... change. [3 sec.] okay. and ... what about work permit for it. anything like that? do I need to get something at the Auslandsamt or? /Interviewer/ perfect. /Interviewer/ <mhm, okay> /Interviewer/ right ... sure, cause it's just I'm going to get my residence permit probably some time this week so I *just need to tick a box or something*... okay. okay, so I think that's possibly it. [laughs slightly] not that I can think of. ... you're looking maybe for British English or American English or ...? /Interviewer/ <mhm> right [laughs] that would be working separately anyway, ... right. [3 sec.] okay. /Interviewer/ no problem [laughs slightly].

I 23f

Sex: female
Age: 21
Origin: Champaign-Urbana, Illinois, USA

1. As far as what do I study ... as a major? umm well, okay, so I'm from Champaign-Urbana, Illinois. I study ... in ... Rock Island, Illinois in the (Quad Cities) at a college called Augustiana College. ... and I am majoring in German ... as a language and political science. I also have two maj - umm two minors umm ... women studies ... and economics. /Interviewer: mhm/ ja. [laughs slightly] /Interviewer: okay/ it's funny, I have to think about what they're - what I say in English. how do I call those. it's been a while. [laughs]

2. Umm ... it's something I always wanted to do, ... and I thought since I knew German, ... I could ... try Germany, but, ... I don't know I've always wanted to travel and live somewhere else to see what the culture's like.

3. Oh, well, ... umm I'm patient and I really do like helping people, and helping them figure things out, ... and I'm not really shy as far as ... speaking in front of lot's of people goes so, ... yeah microphones are something different, but ... as far as just people, it's okay.

4. Umm [3 sec.] is ... I - I like to talk, ... [laughs slightly] that's one, umm [2 sec.] yeah, I'm very patient, ... and I like explaining things to people.

5. Ooooh, ... my strengths are that I'm pretty reliable. I - if I say I'll show up, I'll show up, and I'll be on time, ... umm, my weaknesses, ... would be [2 sec.] umm [2 sec.] oh that's really a good question. [2 sec.] I'm not saying I don't have any. umm ... when I'm really tired or something I get confused really easily and ... I don't always speak very ... clearly, which would - might be hard for the students, ... in the tutorial.

6. [3 sec.] well, ... the more I've been in Germany the more chances I've had to ... help other people with English and to teach other people. ... and I'm really interested in seeing what it's like ... to lead a group ... with pronunciation and ... I really I really enjoy teaching, that's something I didn't think before I came here that I would really like. ... but ... I might wanna pursue teaching, so just the experience itself is something I'm really, really interested in.

7. [3 sec.] umm … it doesn't matter, when I work with others though I tend to take more of a leadership role, [2 sec.] but I could do either way it's okay.

8. [3 sec.] well, … I'd see if maybe I could get them to open up, … but if … that doesn't work, then I just … let them alone. … umm that's how I am when I'm in a bad mood I don't want people to talk to me. so if … they're not cooperating then … this is their education and I'll just do my job.

9. [2 sec.] umm [2 sec.] publicly okay. you know back in my room, when I'm alone, … it's a different matter. but I try and improve on what I'm criticised about.

10. Umm aside from a few speech classes, … and a few … play performances back home, … not really, I haven't done a lot of public speaking, … but … it's [2 sec.] - I can - I have no trouble speaking in front of ten or twelve people. … though when it's … ten or twelve HUNdred people then I'd get really nervous.

11. Oh you're making it sound! [laughs slightly] I think so! [laughs] yeah I think I can handle it. … yeah.

12. How many people would be in the classes? / Interviewer/ oh, well yeah … [laughs slightly] okay. and … as far as lesson plans. you said that you had materials. so is that all set for us as the tutor - the tutors? /Interviewer / <okay, mhm, aha> now, I'll be doing it American though. I mean I know a lot of people here study in - in Great Britain or Australia or something. is that gonna confuse people do you think? /Interviewer/ <okay, [laughs]> all right. I don't wanna make it harder for anybody. /Interviewer/ and … do we set our own hours, or is there - /Interviewer/ <okay, all right> okay and then the other people can just come. but what if - what if - we have to figure out an hour where everybody can come together? /Interviewer/ <okay, oh!> okay. [2 sec.] *I think that's all my questions.* /Interviewer/ <mhm> okay. [2 sec.] and are these students mostly language students, Kuwi[32] students or *just -* /Interviewer/ <okay> okay. I think that's all my questions then. [laughs] /Interviewer/ oh, thank you very much. … it was nice to finally meet you.

---

32 "Kuwi" is the informal name used for students who are enroled in the course of studies "Kulturwirtschaft – International Cultural and Business Studies" at Passau University.

I 24f

Sex: female
Age: 20
Origin: Derby, GB

1. Okay umm I come from … a town near Derby in the Midlands. and
   I study at the University of Durham. in North England not far from
   Newcastle, and there I study European studies with German, umm …
   that entails … *umm* obviously German umm history, sociology and
   politics, umm [2 sec.] other things I enjoy doing? /Interviewer: yeah./
   umm I enjoy going swimming, reading, listen to music and obviously
   play the flute and saxophone.

2. In Germany. I have to do a year abroad. it's part of my course. and …
   our university - with European Studies has three partner universities in
   … Germany, Würzburg, Augsburg and Passau. and … Passau looked
   really nice … and so I decided to come here. [laughs slightly] … and
   I really like it. [laughs slightly]

3. Umm. … since I've been here, I've started doing intercambio, … I've
   … helped with … umm - there is a couple of girls who had their …
   English final oral … exams last week. … and so we met with them …
   every day, … helped them with their English, helped them prepare the
   topics. umm … I've also got English Literature A-level … from home,
   so I have quite a wide vocabulary, … I'm quite widely read, umm …
   and I've also got some teaching practice. not - I've done two umm
   working experiences in England. in primary schools, … and also I
   used to teach flute and saxophone. that's why I - so - although they're
   not … teaching language … I have some kind of basic background
   knowledge … of … how to … react *and things.*

4. Umm … okay. [2 sec.] I hope I am quite personable, so … I'm …
   quite easy to get on with, quite relaxed. … but I don't mind correcting
   people. I hope that people would correct me when I make mistakes in
   German. … so … I like helping people. I like seeing people improve …
   and making sure that they say things properly, and [2 sec.] just that I
   am friendly and … I - I can get on with (*almost*) everybody.

5. [laughs slightly] okay. umm … my strengths are … that … I … get
   on well with most people, … I can … get on with different kinds of

people, from countries, backgrounds, ... it's not a problem for me, umm ... also I enjoy working quite hard, ... we're meeting new people a lot. that's really what I enjoy. umm [2 sec.] what else? ... and yeah. I enjoy helping people. umm weaknesses [5 sec.] umm [2 sec.] weaknesses that apply - that would apply [3 sec.] /Interviewer/ okay umm [laughs] [2 sec.] *it's so hard unless I - I'll tell you a lot* [laughs slightly] umm ... sometimes I'm a little bit ... unorganized but I try to be. when things have to be done. I'm organized but I tend to be a bit [2 sec.] unorganized sometimes, ... umm [3 sec.] and other weaknesses [4 sec.] umm [laughs slightly] I have weaknesses, [laughs slightly] but ... I can't think of them.

6. Okay it REALLY interests me. umm ... just basically helping people. I love helping people. ... improve their language and ... four hours a week ... is ideal because it's - ... it will help me as well. it means I get to meet new people from Germany, which is really great and [2 sec.] umm the money, when I saw it, that wasn't really an issue. I was more interested in ... doing that ( ) job as practice and something to put on my ... CV, ... than ... earning the money. ... umm [2 sec.] I'd just be interested to find out if the times are ... set before. ... if it's four hours that are umm set per week and then ... umm the times that have to be done. [2 sec.] but other than that I'd really really like to do it [laughs slightly]

7. Umm [4 sec.] there's nothing that [2 sec.] umm ... the only thing is it's a contract that we have to sign. and it's a contract for twelve months ... or ... no? /Interviewer/ okay [laughs slightly] then that's no problem [laughs slightly] I'm here for - there's only ten days and over ... Christmas when I'm not here so

8. Umm ... both. ... I've done umm - it's part of my course in England. we have to do two group projects. we have to do one over year. ... and so I really enjoy working as part of a team and taking on different roles ... in a team, and I also umm ... last year in college at university I was a member of the liaison committee. For students who live out. so we worked together on lots of projects umm ... organized parties and information people who lived outside of college. so ... I really do enjoy working as a team. umm ... but yeah. I (also did - can) work independently.

9. Umm ... just remember to keep calm. ... and to be quite light-hearted. ... and not get angry with the kids. there's no point. ... it won't ... solve any problems, it won't help anybody, ... umm [2 sec.] just to try and ... yeah remain light-hearted. help them as best you can. ... and ... keep calm. ... and not get everybody ... even more angry [laughs]

10. Umm ... I think I can take it (well) - I like hearing ... - if ... somebody has something to say to me then I like to hear it. because I hope that ... I can then improve myself or improve the way that I do things, ... and so ... I wouldn't be angry if someone said to me I don't like the way you do this ... that I'd be pleased to hear.

11. Umm ... for our German oral exam last year we had to do a fifteen minute presentation ... for the class. ... on a chosen topic. and also ... last year I was part of - when I was a member of the livers' out committee, I had to give a presentation. on the area of the city where I lived. umm ... to all the first year students. ... in our college ... and [2 sec.] but no. I don't - it doesn't bother me ... speaking in public. I don't ... mind it.

12. Yeah. I'd like to do the best that I can. I'd really like to do it. ... mhm. /Interviewer/ umm we talked the - the contract's only for the semester, umm and I'd just like to know ... when the hours are. - if /Interviewer/ <okay sure, mhm, okay, yeah sure, right> and ... how many students was it? about ten. /Interviewer/ <okay, yeah> and what level of ... English do they have? /Interviewer/ <oh alright, sure, a long time [laughs slightly], okay, yeah> that's fine yeah. that was ... all my questions. /Interviewer/ mhm. /Interviewer/ no I don't think so. /Interviewer/ okay thank you very much. [laughs slightly]

I 25f

Sex: female
Age: 21
Origin: Kent, GB

1. Okay umm I come from Kent. umm I live about an hour away from London, ... [2 sec.] umm I ... went to a ... girls' grammar school, ... until the age of 18 and then I went to ... Durham University, in the North of England. umm where I've been for three years. and umm I've been doing a ... degree. in German and linguistics. so umm ... I had to do ... a year abroad, which is how I come to be studying in Passau. [laughs slightly] umm so I started my year abroad this year, so I have two semesters to do in Passau, studying ... German as a foreign language. umm ... and then I'll go back to England to do my final year ... in Durham. ... umm [9 sec.] [laughs]

2. Umm I think my interest in German started when I was ... quite small. umm I used to have [2 sec.] umm ... lodgers staying in house. ... - in my house at home. umm who were studying ... English, so they wanted to umm be in a family situation and ... learn English. ... from ... everyday. umm and umm [3 sec.] so ... I had a lot of contact. ... and most of them came from Bavaria. so I think that's where my [laughs slightly] - the link came. so when I had to choose my - where I want to do my year abroad ... Passau was ... an obvious choice. I hadn't actually been to Passau before I arrived on the train [laughs slightly] ... about seven weeks ago, but ... umm ... it was a bit of a risk. [laughs slightly] but I was really glad I ... took it. I'm really enjoying it at the moment. It's really ... *really good.*

3. ... umm I've ... taught catechism in a ... church. so Sunday School. for quite a few years in England. umm ... dealing with ... older ... not just small children so older children who ... were able to interact. so ... that should help. umm [3 sec.] in ... Durham I've taken the role as a - a kind of mentor for other students who've just started at the university, particularly in the language center. umm helping them out. umm holding umm [3 sec.] umm help - k - kind of help-hours where they can ... bring their problems to me and ... (save) to discussion. ... dealing with people in that way. umm ... I also ... umm did some - [2 sec.] this kind

of intercambio … situation with umm some Passau students who were … studying in Durham University last year. umm /Interviewer/ the intercambio? well it's this … cambio /Interviewer/ cam/bi/o … when you have a pa - umm I'm not sure what it's called exactly - where you have a partner. umm … a speaking partner. … and you just go for an hour or so over coffee and just … chat. so it's … artificial umm friend-ship [laughs slightly] chatting situation … mhm. [laughs slightly] so I've - I've done that with quite a few students umm at home. … and we shared umm linguistic problems and tried to help each other out in our language learning. … that would be … *quite helpful.* … umm

4. Umm I'm [3 sec.] - like to talk, quite outgoing, I'd like to think I'd umm be able to [2 sec.] be approachable … for other students, if they *have problems.* I think it's always very - it's always umm - … for me anyway, I always feel quite … intimidated in a foreign language. definitely my first six weeks in Passau really changed me a lot. umm so I think I'd find it a lot easier to understand how … difficult it is in a foreign language [laughs slightly] and umm … hopefully be able to … *help.* [laughs slightly]

5. Umm [8 sec.] I think my strengths would be … umm [5 sec.] I think I'm fairly down to earth. umm able to … converse and [5 sec.] - I like meeting new people so that wouldn't be - would be *easy to* … get on with straight away umm [6 sec.] weaknesses umm [4 sec.] that's hard [laughs] umm [laughs slightly] [8 sec.] umm [5 sec.] I'm told I laugh too much in conversations, [laughs] I would have to control my laughter as (then) my English came out in a [laughs] … understand-able manner [laughs slightly]. umm [7 sec.] organization's always been a strong point. … I'm quite an organized person. I like everything to be neat and tidy [laughs slightly]. umm [6 sec.] and then umm [2 sec.] umm hard working. quite dedicated to … study and … especially now that I've had this opportunity to come to Germany I really want to make the most of it.

6. *Umm* [4 sec.] umm … in Durham I've been studying umm … linguistics. … for English. umm in particular we looked at acquisition of foreign language. umm from child's first language acquisition to problems ex-perienced by … older students. so … it'd be very interesting for me. I did a study of … umm … accuracy problems … the German … learners

of English ... and how the - umm ... the - how ones ... umm inaccuracy is related to the fi - to their native language. ... and I found that very - that correlation very interesting. umm ... so that would be a - an interesting ... studies to continue with. umm I'm making to [laughs slightly] - looking to it again when I get back for my dissertation. so I'd be very interested in looking at their errors. - what type of errors they're making. /Interviewer/ umm [laughs slightly] umm [6 sec.] (*umm what'd that be?*) I'd be interested in making the - ... just more umm friendships and getting to know more people. ... umm least umm [laughs slightly] [6 sec.] obviously the [2 sec.] - the main ... objective of ... being able to communicate in a language is to actually communicate. so I'd hope that free flowing conversation rather than ... ( ) *error correction* ( )

7. [3 sec.] umm ... I enjoy teamwork. [2 sec.] umm I like to ... organize myself so that I'm in a situation where I can work effectively in the team. so in that respect ... some ... umm working ... *individually*. but teamwork is definitely more my ... thing. [laughs slightly] umm I like ... interacting with others, getting ideas of other people. *that kind of thing*.

8. [3 sec.] *umm* I think you have to find a [2 sec.] basis that - a ground where they can ... feel that they want to communicate. where they want to ... work. if it's something that they're not interested in, if it's - they're having a bad day and they'd rather do something else, then that's going to be more productive than ... what the original plan was. so I think you have to be flexible. [3 sec.] *it's quite important to* ... take mood into consideration maybe [laughs slightly] umm ... hopefully we'd be on - umm ... we'd be able to communicate well enough for them to tell me what they wanted to be doing. ... so it wouldn't be as though I was imposing something ... on them.

9. ... umm ... I think it's helpful and ... I'd ... take it into consideration. ... umm ... I wouldn't take it personally. [laughs slightly] ... I'd try not to, and to - umm ... consider it. to ... better what I'm doing. umm ... *to improve*. (*that's it*)

10. Yes I've ... umm done ... seven presentations in front of ... a thousand people. one was in front of ... just over a thousand. umm when I was at school I ... was ... involved in ... giving the speeches on speech day, ... umm [2 sec.] I've - I'm actually a cox. umm for ... - for rowing

boats. ... so I speak with the microphone ... and control the boat. so ... in that ... situation tone of voice, speed of ... umm what you're saying ... is all very important. the way you say it. ... pronunciation ... is very *important. ... for making the boat go faster.* [laughs slightly] *so I think that would be helpful.* [laughs slightly]

11. *Yes* I'm very confident. [laughs]

12. umm what kind of - ... umm I'm not entire clear which students it would be. ... and what kind of level they'd be at. /Interviewer/ <okay, mhm> umm [7 sec.] and I've forgotten how often it was that we ... would meet. /Interviewer/ four times four times. yeah. /Interviewer/ yes okay. *that's* -   and how many ... students would be in each? /Interviewer/ <okay, mhm, [laughs]> /Interviewer/ *no I think that's all.* /Interviewer/ *okay* [laughs] thank you

I 26m

Sex: male
Age: 20
Origin: Leeds, GB

1. Okay I come from Leeds in the North of England and I study at the University of Durham. ... in it's - it's not too far away from Newcastle, ... and there I study European Studies with German. ... and so it's a multidisciplinary course where ... you study politics, history ... yeah sociology but ... in my second year I've slightly ... changed my course so I now study mainly languages and history. [2 sec.] and learn about the institutions of Europe ... *and* [3 sec.] I - yeah I'm very fond of foreign language learning and ... I ... - partially due to my background with having Polish parents so ... umm... I can speak Polish and ... I've just started last year to learn Russian. [7 sec.] okay.

2. In Germany? umm ... well partially it was part of my degree - like - ... umm doing a European Studies degree you have to spend a year abroad in Germany and ... I just umm - I felt the experience would be ... almost invaluable to both like my self esteem and .... umm just the cultural experience of living abroad for a year, it' s not something which many people can ... experience.

3. Well ... I'm not entirely sure if I have any such qualifications which would help me as a tutor. but *yeah* [4 sec.] I'm sorry I'm [laughs slightly] ... /Interviewer/ yeah okay.

4. Well I'm ... quite patient with people. and (so) *yeah* I ... usually get on ... quite well with other people as well and [2 sec.] *I don't know* I [laughs]

5. Well my strengths are that I'm punctual and ... quite organized however my ... main weak - weakness has to be my self-confidence and ... I'm not particularly confident ... - like speaking in front of a large group of people. [3 sec.] *okay.*

6. Umm the aspect which interests me the most is just umm [2 sec.] kind of umm [2 sec.] the learning - like overall how to - like ... teach ... a bunch of - umm sorry a group of students and ... yeah the ... experiences you can learn from this and ... the learning about the difficulties Germans have in pronouncing certain English words and ... umm

yeah ... whether at all it's possible for them to ... actually ... s - like say these words - like ... properly and ... also the things which ... are probably least - of least interest are *I don't know* umm [2 sec.] perhaps repetition in ... yeah the ... teaching. ... /Interviewer/ yes. [laughs slightly]

7. Umm ... I like working ... both because umm ... it was part of my course we had to do a group project which ... umm so I can see the advantages and disadvantages of both mainly ... relying upon other people is ... not ... always very... good. *well* depending on how well they work as a group. umm in general I ... prefer to work alone. *yeah.*

8. Yes [laughs] ... right umm [4 sec.] partially umm ... *I don't know* umm ... it's quite a tough question. [laughs] well umm ... I would probably just carry on with the class as usual and then after the lesson has ended I would ... take them to one side and ask ... if they have a problem with my teaching methods or ... if the - they are unsatisfied with anything

9. Umm usually quite well. like I ... - I'd be very happy to hear what people think of me and ... yeah ... whether I'm any good or not. ... [laughs]

10. Umm ... apart from ... presentations at university I don't really have any experience with speaking in public but ... I am usually quite nervous to ... start with

11. Umm [3 sec.] I'm not sure to be - to be honest I ... yeah I'm not entirely sure whether ... I would be the - like ideal person for this job. ... mainly due to self-confidence.

12. Umm ... no not really w*ell yeah* [4 sec.] no. /Interviewer/ okay okay thank you

I 27m

Sex: male
Age: 21
Origin: Solihull, GB

1. Okay well I'm originally from Wales umm Cardiff. ... umm ... lived there until I was ... seven years old. moved to Solihull ... *where* there's dad's job. ... and lived there for ... almost nine years ... that's right. did my GCSE's and ... pre - grew up as a teenager. umm ... moved back to Cardiff to do my A-levels. and ... attend Cardiff University where I'm studying German and law. umm I'm studying law here also in Passau umm [2 sec.] umm [laughs] what else about myself? umm ... I enjoy sports umm ... enjoy socializing ... possibly a bit too much but umm [laughs] *that's all good* umm [2 sec.] *what else?* ... umm [2 sec.] what umm - ... other things should I ... [laughs slightly] reveal? ... I'm not too sure.

2. In Ge - well umm as part of ... the German course in Cardiff we have to ... come to Germany for a year. ... and (also) improve the language. umm ... and I chose Passau because the reputation is good with the law department umm ... my dad's quite umm ... internet ... - in a business world umm - works ... maybe ... three or four times a month in Germany ... and umm (everybody else) said ... that umm - that Passau is a good place to come for law. so ... it seemed like the right thing to do ... umm ... *yeah* ... [laughs]

3. As a tu... - well my umm my study of ... the English language ... would hope [laughs] - would help quite a lot. umm ... what qualifications? - I mean I've [2 sec.] - umm obviously with the - with the languages. ... that always helps at communication skills. umm both are with communication. umm ... I've been captain to my school rugby side ... for - for four years so ... I'm used to having to ... shout at - [laughs slightly] not shout at people in a class obviously but ... get - get a point across. umm ... and also my umm - at my school in Solihull. I was part of a programme where ... umm ... the oldest students helped umm ... umm some younger German - umm students studying German umm who were struggling so I've done a - a bit of umm - it wasn't really teaching but ... - but as a .... as a tutor helped there so ... I think that would come in quite handy.

4. Well personal skills. ... umm I think I ... - I'm quite easy to communicate with ... I like to think I'm quite friendly [laughs] umm ... I've never really had any trouble ... umm [2 sec.] in communicating with people. umm ... I'm also quite patient. umm never used to be but ... I've umm been living with my brother and his - and his son. my nephew. for the past umm few years so ... [laughs] you become a lot more patient when there's a - when there's a little child running round ... umm ... so ... yeah I think umm ... I'd be ... a good candidate ... *I'd hope.*

5. Strengths and weaknesses umm ... that's a tough one. ... umm ... again *umm* I (*just kind of*) *think* ... I'm quite easy to ... - to talk to, quite approachable. umm ... I think as far as the ... pronunciation goes I don't really have ... any sort of ... accent umm ... because I haven't ... (*really*) stayed long enough in any [laughs] - one place in the ... UK ... so ... I - I think I'd be quite easy to understand. umm [2 sec.] yeah ... umm [3 sec.] weaknesses. I think I'm a ... bit too optimistic. ... about things which can ... develop into naivety. [laughs] but umm ... I try to curb that as much as I can. umm ... I think - I think I'm quite organized and ... quite down to earth so [2 sec.] I'm trustworthy I suppose ... - or I'd hope. ... *what people say ... umm ... yeah* [laughs slightly]

6. Umm ... most well it's just meeting ... new people. umm ... I've been meeting quite a few ... through ... umm AEGEE's. umm AEGEE schemes ... and umm various trips to ... Munich and Berlin etcetera umm ... but these were all foreign students ... and it'd be nice to meet some - some German students as well. ... umm ... and also ... have the option to socialize with them outside of ... the class and improve my German and their English at the same time ... umm ... obviously as well as the ... jobs are getting paid is always ... something to look forward to ... umm ... it can be very helpful ... as far as umm lifestyle ... goes in Passau ... umm ... and plus I've got quite a bit of free time because ... my obligations for my home university only entail umm ten hours of lectures per week and a seminar ... so I've got ... quite a ... quite a lot of free time which ... I don't have that much to do with ...umm ... I have two dissertations to write. ... but ... that's not gonna take up all my time I umm ... I just think

I'm - would get bored if [laughs] you're just ... sitting in Mensa[33] and ... - and that sort of thing. so definitely just having ... something to do - something to occupy myself with. ... umm something worthwhile as I'm obviously ... helping others umm ... least ... umm [5 sec.] I'm not really sure I suppose. ... if it ... - well (*I'll*) see if it in -... umm ... intruded on the timetable. that would be ... - that would be a problem. that's the only thing I'd be worried about but apart from that there's nothing I'm ... - I wouldn't look forward to about (but I would) think ... umm I' m sure ... all the students are ...very nice and ... [laughs] and approachable so ... *yeah*

7. Umm very much with others yeah ... umm ... as I said umm as far as the sports go I've always - always played sports and worked umm [2 sec.] in -... as umm - in part of a team. umm ... as - as well with law umm since I've been studying ... we ...'*re* congregating in study groups and umm it just makes life a lot easier when there's umm - there's more heads. ... to umm ... consider topics and ... - and issues ... umm ... so yeah I'm very much a ... team person. ... *umm* ... *well* I suppose I CAN work individually if [laughs] - if it needs to be but ... yeah ... I certainly find studying with others and working with others as a lot more beneficial.

8. [laughs slightly] well I try to be as umm accommodating as possible. umm ... I know there are trials and tribulations that student life can ... - can bring. mainly hangovers and problems with respected partners. [laughs] so umm ... yeah I think umm ... I'd be ... quite willing to ... - to help out on any - any level I was able to. and I act as a bit of a social worker amongst my umm circle of friends back home. umm ... I've quite a lot of experience with [2 sec.] all aspects of life. ... so umm ... umm ... I'm - I'd hopefully be able to ... - be able to help out and ... - and if that wasn't the case ... then umm ... I would certainly not hassle them and [laughs] just - just let them go on ... do the wrong thing and ... just be there. - and be any support *when I could*.

9. Criticism well ... I hope I handle criticism very well. umm [2 sec.] I mean it's ... part - part of teaching. umm ... umm *you know* especially

---

with - with languages you're always been told ...what - what you're not supposed to say and how to pronounce things *and* ... - *and* that's and umm ... very well. it's the same with most subjects I've studied as well umm ... *you know you're always* - you're always being given criticism. as long as it's ... constructive criticism and it's something you can work off I find it ... very beneficial. *umm ... so* - so I certainly wouldn't take it badly. [laughs]

10. Speaking in public. umm [2 sec.] I haven't done any public speaking as such ... umm ... apart from umm ... giving speeches as ... - as the umm ... captain of the rugby side. ... umm accepting awards ... that sort of thing. but never actually any [2 sec.] umm ... fully fledged public speaking as it were. umm ... but *you know* I don't really have any ... - any problems with doing it. umm ... mostly ... you get a bit nervous but ... I think that's a good thing umm ... yeah umm as far as - as ... standing up in front of groups and talking ... goes I've got no problem with that at all. umm ... part of the law scheme in Cardiff is ... umm ... - with the seminars ... getting up and ... - and delivering your ... - your opinion on ... whatever question may have been set ... to a group of umm ... twenty to thirty people. ... umm ... and doing that week in week out you get used to it. umm ... so ... yeah I don't think ... *I'd* ... struggle too much *doing it*.

11. Mhm /Interviewer/ YES certainly. I'd hope so! umm ... I can't see any ... - any umm ... real problems in ... - in doing so. ... umm ... also it depends on a good relationship with the students but umm ... (*as*) I said I think I'm ... friendly enough and approachable enough to ... - to build up a good relationship and ... - and hopefully work well with them.

12. Umm [4 sec.] only really as far as ... timetable issues go. when the umm - when the lessons would be /Interviewer/ oh we'd be /Interviewer/ <yeah, okay, right> yeah well ... umm that's ... - that's about all I think. [laughs slightly] /Interviewer/ okay thank you.

I 28f

Sex: female
Age: 20
Origin: Tacoma, Washington State, USA

1. Mhm umm ... well I come from originally? Walnut Creek California,
   ... but I study in Tacoma Washington, ... at the University of Puget
   Sound, ... and umm there I am a member of the bachelor's programme
   of foreign language and international affairs. and umm ... my central
   studies ha(ve) been ... the German language, ... European politics and
   international business. ... so umm ... the university is actually a very
   small umm liberal arts university, so in the tradition of liberal arts,
   umm in the last two years of my studies I've just taken general courses
   of English literature, biology, sociology, and I am just now starting
   umm to in - intensely study my - my subjects and I figured ... the best
   way to ... learn about Europe and the German language is to come to
   Passau for a year. so

2. Umm I ... lived in Germany before. I took part in ... a - a school foreign
   exchange, it was with the organisation Rotary International, and ...
   umm I was a guest at ... a school in ... Göttingen. Germany. in Nied-
   ersachsen. and so I stayed there with umm three different host families,
   umm throughout the course of one full year. so umm I just ... umm -
   this experience I just fell in love with it. it's ... a ... great experience for
   me especially since I was umm very young and I took to the language
   very well. and I enjoy speaking German and ... studying German so
   ... I figured that umm it'd be best to come back to Germany [laughs
   slightly] and study for a full year if I could. [laughs] *yeah*

3. Umm well I've worked with umm students before, ... umm in a very
   small ... umm ... private company, umm it's a reading company. and
   ... umm they teach umm young children ... umm often form the ages
   of ... umm seven or eight to ... fourteen ... how to read. so I've umm
   helped out a little bit, because the company umm belongs to a family
   friend of mine, ... umm but my most qualifying experience would be
   ... umm the - probably the last month [laughs slightly] that I've been
   here I've been working with a - a student she's ... umm ... an older
   student, ... she decided to ... umm ... go to the ... foreign language

school and ... study English there, to improve her career ... o - options. and umm so I've been working with her ... about two or three times a week ... umm ... for the last three or four weeks. ... and umm I ('ve) learned a lot with working ... - umm with her and she's at a - at a beginning level. I'd say umm as far as speaking and comprehension goes. umm ... so that's definitely ... that's umm [laughs slightly] been my best experience so far in - *in teaching but*

4. Umm personal qualifications? well ... umm ... I like to work with people very much, [laughs] umm I enjoy umm ... *umm* working ... umm in groups, so ... umm if I had a small group of students umm that I could work with, that's umm - that's ... the best environment for me. umm I'm ... most receptive in a - in such an environment and ... umm I like discussions in - in small groups. and so I think that I'll be most successful ... umm with a small group of students because that's ... umm - that's something that I really like, and that I really enjoy. ... so ... umm other than that, personal qualifications? umm ... [laughs slightly] umm ... (*I'm*) not sure I like - *umm* like I said I just like working with people and I'm interested to see ... umm ... umm how ... the students most successfully learn ... another language because that helps myself as well since I'm still learning German and umm I'm interested in learning techniques ... umm because my mother's a kindergarten teacher so ... I have /Interviewer/ a kindergarten teacher. mhm so I have ... a little knowledge of ... how people you know ... use to pick up umm ... you know the sounds and ... you know the basics ... of learning. but umm ... - but I'm really ... interested in - in finding (*it*) out for myself, and I think ... you know in - ... the opportunity to be in umm - to teach a small group of students would probably the best way to do that [laughs slightly]

5. Mmh ... my strengths and my weaknesses - my - I'd say ... umm ... one of my strengths is working with other people. especially in a small group. umm ... I've ... umm ... - as far as ... umm other jobs that I've had ... before umm I've almost always worked in a small restaurant. either a small café or a small restaurant or a small bakery over the last four or five years. and ... umm ... I like working in small groups and being able ... umm to ... cooperate and find a - a way ... that everyone can be the most successful in whatever they are doing so umm ... I

think I'm pretty good at that I - and I really enjoy ... helping people umm ... in a - ... in a small group and umm [2 sec.] I think that's - that's *definitely a very strong ... personal quality of mine.* one of my weaknesses ... is that umm [2 sec.] I [2 sec.] - I ... don't - I don't deal very well with confrontation. ... so I deal very well with constructive criticism, but umm if umm there's a situation where I need to confront someone about a - a major issue, oftentimes I have trouble with that.

6. Umm [2 sec.] (*let's see*) probably ... most, it would definitely be a chance to - to work with German students. umm ... just to get to know ... German students, I'm assuming ... umm they'll be mostly German students. umm because I've umm plenty of international ... umm ... friends. other international students that are ... - are studying here at Passau. what I'm really looking forward to ... getting to know some other German students. and hearing what's umm ... umm their ... - hearing what they think about the English language and what - where they have trouble and ... umm not only with something like pronunciation umm but as far as more general concepts or rules of the language. and umm ... I'm really - I'm really interested in that and I'm hoping umm to make some good ... personal connections so ... umm I can ... out - maybe outside of class just speak with the students freely and improve my German as well. /Interviewer: okay and what interests you least?/ umm [3 sec.] that's hard to say! I'm umm - I'm not sure about ... the hours? umm being four hours umm ... four hours of class a week, umm since I also have another ... umm English student I'm worried that umm the - the two will conflict. umm ... but *that's probably it.*

7. ... umm ... mmh *that's a good question.* ... I'd say with - with others. ... *with other teachers.* ... because I think umm ... yeah the more the merrier, is it? [laughs] *it's a phrase but* ... I think oftentimes if there is more than one teacher then ... you can recognize each other's strengths and weaknesses and then fill in the gaps. so that the students will get more of a ... umm - ... ( ) just more umm ... - more quality teaching then all around.

8. Mmh I'd probably ... try and lighten the subject matter? ... umm ... if we're going over something ... umm ... - either something very basic and maybe some people are bored ... or umm ... - they don't - they

just - it's just not necessarily material that umm … - that they - they - they wanna work on at that time, I'd either try and make the subject ma - the … subject matter entertaining, by using … silly examples … or umm … - or … umm maybe do an activity that would kind of loosen them up. … cause if it's a small group then it's easy … umm to say "okay we're gonna take … a few minute break" and then … we'll have … a small … discussion or something that isn't directly related to what we were … working on before. but still on the same … vein … either … the discussion will be held in English or we'll just practice some … fun vocabulary or slang or something *if they're interested in that*. … *but* … something to loosen them up. [laughs slightly]

9. Umm [2 sec.] fairly well, … I'd say. umm [2 sec.] I take criticism … seriously, and … although … it's - it's never fun to [laughs] umm - to receive criticism, oftentimes umm … I'll - I'll think about it and … whoever is giving me criticism I'll always ask them how I can … im- prove … whatever I'm doing wrong. I think constructive criticism is definitely the most umm effective type of criticism. so umm [2 sec.] if … a student will come up to me after class and say "you know I didn't really underst - umm understand this umm how you explained it maybe you could explain it a different way" then … you know I often … talk about the - umm … about … whatever the teaching-style or the specific manner so … umm … - so the next time when I deal … with material … that's *related, then I can teach in a more effective way. so*

10. … umm … I speaking in public? that's umm [2 sec.] I prefer umm … mmh [3 sec.] I prefer umm … smaller groups, [laughs slightly] if I speak in public, umm I think it really depends … umm (*on*) the audience. and what I'm speaking about. … umm … I've … umm - I have a fair amount of experience both in school, …at the university … umm giving reports, … umm … mmh … yeah - giving reports, umm speaking in class, giving an opinion … and then umm also giving presentations, … not only at the university but privately for example umm … my foreign exchange through the Rotary International Organisation I've given a few speeches about my experience there … to groups of either umm Rotary Clubs, … umm which were about 30, 40 people … or umm [2 sec.] also to smaller groups of students that are interested in the exchange program. so … I have a - a fair amount of e - experience … *in public speaking*.

11. Mhm

12. Yes [laughs] umm ... I am curious umm ... about the - the students what they're going - umm what level they're at? and you mentioned in your e-mail that it's umm mostly ... umm first semester students. /Interviewer/ mhm ... and ... umm ... being first semester students ... here at the university does it mean that they've had any previous ... umm ... umm English lessons, correct? /Interviewer/ <okay mhm great yeah> and umm ... so ... as [2 sec.] - as far as umm the material? is there any recommended? umm /Interviewer/ <mhm, okay> umm [3 sec.] and umm ... the students are just umm ... - they're taking general English classes now, or ... are most of them considering English either for ... Kuwi[34]? ... or /Interviewer/ <okay, great, mhm> umm ... you mentioned that umm it's four hours a week? and that the students can choose ... however many hours they want to go in ... /Interviewer/ then one hour ... okay. /Interviewer/ <mhm, okay> and umm ... yeah I'm curious about what sort of material you have [laughs slightly] because umm ... with the student that I'm working on now umm ... - that I'm working with umm usually she has homework that she brings back from her foreign language school and ... umm then ... I'm going over umm - she'll read something aloud and when I ... you know ... if I notice that there's a certain ... umm ... group of letters that she always umm pronoun -mispronounces, then we can work on that and I'll make a list of similar words something like that, but that's kind of - ... I'm ... working off of what she's already ... learning in school, so I'm curious as far as umm ... - just kind of where to start [laughs] / Interviewer/ <mhm, great> great ... okay that's umm - that gives me confidence so I know where - that I have a place to - to go off of. okay [2 sec.] *great* ... umm [2 sec.] how - how big are the groups going to be? ( ) /Interviewer/ five to ten? ... that's great ... okay /Interviewer/ [laughs] yeah sixteen ... that'd be ... - that'd be awesome. [laughs] *so ... yeah* and umm this will continue umm ... for this semester? / Interviewer/ umm until? umm /Interviewer/ <mhm> and are - are all

---

34 "Kuwi" is the informal name used for students who are enroled in the course of studies "Kulturwirtschaft – International Cultural and Business Studies" at Passau University.

the students from your classes? or … /Interviewer/ <mhm> and … umm … do you … umm … - do you ask that they give umm … umm verbal tests? or spoken tests? … verbal tests! I'm trying to … directly translate from German [laughs slightly] /Interviewer/ <mhm> okay … which is great. cause … umm … when I was in - when I went to school at the Gymnasium, I - umm the English teacher … umm often just … gave lectures and there wasn't a - necessarily a lot of spoken English in the class. and … umm he did ask questions once in a while, … but … the only people that raised their hands were the people that already had experience with the … English. … either they'd already done some sort of exchange or [2 sec.] so *yeah but umm … great … that's great I think umm* … I'm really looking forward to it. [laughs] /Interviewer/ yeah and umm when would you like … the classes to start? /Interviewer/ <mhm, great, right> and I'm curious what do you teach here at the University … of Passau? specifically umm … like what courses are you teaching this semester? /Interviewer/ <mhm, okay, that's great> [laughs slightly] I'm not ve - I don't know much about it but [laughs] … to be honest … it's always like to - you know … [laughs] *yeah okay* … well … - well I'm glad that I - I got to meet you ( ), thank you for inviting me for the interview, I'm so sorry I was late but /Interviewer/ [laughs slightly] in case we meet again, I know where your office is. so [laughs] /Interviewer/ great.

I 29f

Sex: female
Age: 20
Origin: Dublin, Ireland

1. Well I come from Dublin in Ireland, so I'm studying at University College Dublin, and I study a course that's somewhat similar to BWL, but it's ... a little bit more finance and accounting based as opposed to ... Wirtschaft or economics. Umm ... I've been here since September and last summer I went to ... Los Angeles for the summer, just umm - a lot of our students do (it). it's called a J1-Visa, ... just to work for the summer and experience the American culture and ... that sort of thing. so I've been ... away from home for almost an ... entire year, [laughs slightly] and ... I have ... three older brothers and two older sisters, ... so ... I'm the youngest, of six ... umm ... my sister's getting married in ... November, so that's all very exciting. ... and ... next year will be my last year at college, ... I just have one more year ... back in Dublin, ... umm ... I'm really enjoying it here in Passau. I really really like ... the German culture, all people are SO nice. I'm having an amazing year. I didn't ... exactly want to come in the first place. but it was a requirement of our course, and now I'm SO glad that I came. I think everybody should ... have to do it. *it's really really great.*

2. Umm ... well as part of our ... - umm ... secondary school education, which is ... kind of like the Gymnasium and the Abitur, we have to take a foreign language in order to study - study at college, because ... a lot of English speakers don't ... really tend to take (*foreign*) languages and it's ... not always that important, but we have to ... have it at a certain level. so I chose ... German instead of French or Spanish and there (ain't any) things that are available to us, and then umm ... when I was going into college I had the opportunity to go away for a year, and at that stage I'd thought it was a great idea and ... it'd be ... a great experience and ... I just - I thought Germany'd be very nice, and ... I'd gone on an exchange to ... Baden-Baden when I was about ... fourteen? ... and I really really enjoyed it. it was only ... two weeks long but ... *it was ... great.*

3. Umm ... I think ... umm I've worked in four ... clothes shops. and I know that's ... - it's not exactly the - the same idea, but ... when you're

there you have to ... be able to ... speak to customers and approach them, and you have to be able to listen to them and - and speak to them, and I think that's a - a great skill for ... any job really, but e - especially to stand up in front of a class of people and - and speak to them and to be able to just make conversation with people, ... umm as well at ... college - when I was - when I'm studying ... commerce, we have to get up and do presentations, almost ... at least once a month. which is a great skill. cause I know ... - my sister was at college. in the entire time she was there she didn't have to do ... anything like that, ... and she works for Microsoft now and has to do it. ... and the first time she had to get up, she was absolutely terrified. and I'm like oh same old same old. [laughs slightly] *it's all the same at this stage.* so I 'm used to getting up in front of people and - and speaking and ... I think that it'd definitely help if I had to get up in front of a class of people. and ... last term as - as I said we did the ... umm classes, it was any one hour a week. but I got to work with German students, and get to know ... a few German students and ... get to see what it'll be like to teach the class. ... so I was really interested in doing something ... a bit more ... expansive this term.

4. *Mmh* ... umm I think I've always had a - a great interest in the English language, ... now, I read an awful lot and umm I'll be that annoying person that corrects people's grammar when we're out. [laughs slightly] *to whom instead of ... to who isn't it?)* but umm umm ... I think just the - the interest and enthusiasm ... will definitely help. and umm it's definitely something that I wanted to ... try ... and maybe do later on in - in life. I really ... think it could be ... a great experience and ... it's just something I really really wanted to do. and umm ... I know umm one of the guys who did it last term and he ... really enjoyed it. he said ... he probably wouldn't do it again this term but ... to do it once was ... a great experience and ... very interesting.

5. Mmh umm [2 sec.] I'll start with the ... weaknesses then I suppose, I - I think ... the ... - my biggest weakness is that ... I have to be prepared beforehand - I - I don't like to be caught unaware or anything like that I think I have to sit down and sort things out and make sure I know what I'm doing before I get up and do it, so ... it's a little bit difficult that way ... umm ... but ... generally I think one of my strong points

is that I will be organized and will have it done. ... and I ... if - if I say I'm going to do something I will definitely get it done and have it done ... to the best of my abili*ties*. so ... it's kind of ... one that counteracts the other but ... it all kinda works out *in the end* so

6. I think umm ... most of all it's to work with the German students. because as an Erasmus student I do know ... quite a few ... German students, but I don't really get to talk to them. as much as - I - I speak to a lot of French or Spanish and that's a good thing but it's not ... quite the same as speaking with ... the Germans themselves, and I think it would ... give me a look a bit more ... at the German culture? ... and I would get to experience what student life is for them, because it's obviously very different as an Erasmus student and the different (alliances and ... things like that made first so) ... it'd be nice to - to hear and see ... and get to know some more German students, umm ... least is probably [2 sec.] trying to fit in around my timetable, because I have a lot of hours this semester, ...umm ... which - it isn't too bad. I think. umm ... I've most of Thursday and Friday free ... and a - a lot of Monday I've ... Tuesday and Wednesday are quite packed. so the - the worst part of it is trying to fit it around my own studies, ... umm and ... the ... hours that I'll have to prepare just to make sure I - I have ... certain - a lot of times to ... prepare beforehand for the classes *and things like that.*

7. Umm ... I can do ... either actually I enjoy working as part of a team and I've had to do that a lot. especially in ... college we've to do group projects and things and then ... obviously working ... in ... umm clothes shops and things like that we've to ... work together *I think with -* but umm ... I - I don't mind to work - working on my own is *fine also.* so either way ... suits me ... *I'm* quite *easy going that way*

8. Umm ... I think the ... best thing is to keep ... things light-hearted yourself. cause if you are in a good mood, it's going to ... project onto them and if you're in a bad mood it's obviously going to ... project onto them as well, if you try to ... liven up the class a little bit or ... maybe take something that you know interests them or ... that could be a little bit different. umm especially on the days that they don't seem ... to want to do something. umm ... is probably the best way to - to go about it. try and get them more enthusiastic and [2 sec.] maybe go on to the personal level a bit - a bit more

9. I think I take it … quite well, I think this - this term especially because umm umm a lot of people … would correct my German and things like that. and you just learn to - to deal with that and to take it. … umm and … to turn it into a positive thing? just to try to … correct whatever they've … criticized or … whatever they've corrected. try to build from there onwards, … try to make it better.

10. Umm … I think I'm quite confident when I speak in public. I did a lot of … drama classes when I was younger and … I did umm … a lot of singing classes. so I'm well used to getting up on stage and being in front of people. and I don't really mind speaking in front of other people that's - that's fine with me. (so) I think I'm - I think it's one - one part that I'm quite confident with. … is just getting up in front of people.

11. Yeah I think I would be able to … I hope I'd be able to contribute … a lot towards it and I think … it would benefit me as well so it - it would work both ways that I could … help these students and … that I could give a *hundred percent and … I'd like the experience of it. things like that so…*

12. Umm I don't think so, I think umm … I've - I was talking to Kevin before and he … was telling me what he did last term? so … I - I kind of got the inside view of [laughs slightly] - of what happens in class and things like that so it sounded very enjoyable. … he seemed to like it. so … /Interviewer/ no problem [laughs slightly]

I 30m

Sex: male
Age: 22
Origin: Scotland

1. Umm my name is 30[35]. umm ... I'm ... umm 22 ... I was born ... in
    Scotland, ... on an island in the south west ... but my mother is English
    and I've also lived in England as well. umm ... I spent a year living in
    York, in - it's the north - it's northeast of England. and then ... almost a
    year in London. so that was nice. that was before I went to university.
    umm in between school and university yes. umm ... at university at the
    moment I study just German. umm ... in Scotland it's usual to do three
    subjects in your first year. and then two in your second. and then ...
    maybe go down to one subject in the third and fourth year ... umm so I
    did ... French as well in first year. and business as well. but now I'm - I've
    ... stopped doing them so I just do the German *right now*. ... which is
    my - so - favourite subject.

2. Umm ... well it is compulsory for ... the course that I do. I was a lan-
    guage assistant. in Saxony from 2003 to 2004. and having done that I
    may possibly been able to ( ) doing it. it was something I wanted to do
    cause ... well mainly cause *I feel my German needs to improve really.*

3. Umm my job here? yes. umm well I spent nine months teaching Eng-
    lish in Saxony, so I think that should be a big help. umm ... yes. some-
    times it was a little ... stressful. ... when you have a ... entire class of
    year nines or whatever to yourself for ... an hour or two ... *but yes.*
    you sort of - you learn how to cope with it a bit you know? at first I
    was quite ... shy and I was like "No no, please be quiet" but ... you
    really have to speak up to them and yeah ... make sure they listen to
    you and things. but I think in smaller groups that won't be quite so
    bad. ... and then maybe be a little bit more ... enthusiastic here than -
    some of the - umm Grundkurs students (well).

4. *Personal qualifications?* umm ... I've already become a little bit more
    outgoing since living in Germany. umm yes so ... I'm quite outgoing

---

35 The number "30" is used here instead of the first name of the applicant.

now ... talkative ... umm ... I like Germany in general and ... I think it'll be interesting to learn ( ) social perspective of Germany.

5. Umm ... well I'm a bit of a perfectionist. so umm sometimes I spend a bit long trying to get something just right. when really I should sort of ... move on to the next thing that's ( ) ... umm ... I think I'm very t - chatty, outgoing umm yeah good fun perhaps? yeah.

6. Umm ... it'll be ... quite a bit of preparation I should imagine so ... that'll take up some of my time. ... umm I think it'll help my German ... doing it. ... I don't know ... everyone's English in Germany is always so good ( ) but *that'll be good*. the money would be nice *as well*.

7. I think it's easier if you have support from other people. if you have a problem then there's somebody there ... if the - if there's someone who can help you then that's ...you're not on your own and so forth.

8. Umm ... try not to let that affect yourself too much. umm they're not so much in a bad mood with you though just in a bad mood. if they don't want to learn then don't take it too personal.

9. Umm everyone ... in Saxony laughed over my German cause it is so awful. so ... I think ... especially with the younger years, when you're five or you're six, when I umm spoke German to them´. ... it made them more ... willing or feel more confident about speaking English to me. because they realized that my German wasn't perfect so their English doesn't have to be perfect.

10. Umm ... at home on my island I go to church. and umm ... there is meetings every week so ... that's about the only public speaking that I do is to read the - the gospel or whatever in the - in church.

11. I think so yes. I hope so yes *that I'd be*.

12. Umm ... you said small groups about seven or eight or something? /Interviewer/ <yes, *right*> umm ... the material covered does it relate or does that have to relate to anything that they study ... as part of their course or? /Interviewer/ umm ... I don't think so. ... what about things like ... photocopying and stuff? I don't have a printer with me in Germany *just my laptop*. /Interviewer/ <ok>

I 31f

Sex: female
Age: 20
Origin: Scotland, GB

1. Well umm I'm from Scotland, I come from a town just south of Glasgow, it's yeah quite - it's about the same size as Passau, but I study in Sterling, University, which is also very similar to Passau. so that's why I kind of - I chose to come here because ... I thought: "Oh it'd be nice ... to go somewhere." umm ... I study Spanish ... and German. ... in Sterling. so ... for that reason I had to spend ... a ... semester ... in Germany to do something about my German. so [laughs] because otherwise ... it was ... not great [laughs]. but yeah that's ... mostly ... Scotland's yeah really nice ... and ... it's very ... very similar to Bavaria actually. so ... not so - ... not so different.

2. Well firstly because of this - I - I had to do - it's compulsory in my university to spend time. ... and umm ... I ... yeah ... - we - I'd like to come - I wanted to come to Bavaria, because ... umm I've previously worked in ... Austria and I always thought: "Oh yeah well ... you know Bavaria is quite similar to Austria and so and so" ... yep. and I've worked - I worked the last three months in Munich. ... and ... so it was nice to - I thought I could do ... some time in Munich and then just move along ... to - to Passau. ... so yeah ... it's all good at the moment [laughs slightly].

3. With the tutor? well ... at the moment I don't have any formal ... qualifications, but well for the past ... few years or so [laughs slightly] I've been teaching English ... as a foreign language, umm the last - ... last month I taught in the Cambridge Institute, ... in Munich, where ... I was teaching classes umm ... for the adults, ... mostly, ... non-Germans. people who were coming from Eastern Europe and wanted to learn English. and also I taught umm ... umm a holiday course, ... there for children who were coming from - they were preparing for the Abitur, so ... I did - we did classes there. I also normally - I teach ... English in the summer, [laughs slightly] at a camp in Austria, that's why I chose *to come here*. and umm ... I spent one year. ... in Spain also in a high school teaching English there. so ... but as yeah - I have no [laughs] formal qualifications so ... it's all a bit ... strange.

4. What do you mean by pe - just what personal ... qualities? umm ... I don't know. I think ... I [laughs] like to talk [laughs] so I think it would be ... good if it's ... umm - I can give a good impression of my country, and ... the language, ... I'm very proud of being ... a Scottish person and ... I'd like to ... give that back to other people, because I think it's a pity sometimes when ... foreigners learn English, and ... they learn ... it a different ... - a different way and they don't learn about the other parts of English and the other dialects and so on and yeah I think ... I'm quite a ... easy going person and [laughs slightly] easy to go on with so ... I think that should help me hopefully. ... *so we'll see.*

5. Oh ... strengths and weaknesses. ... umm ... my ... weaknesses, let me think ... umm I probably have many but [laughs] umm ... I'm very ... umm ... unsympathetic actually. I would say as a weakness. I'm one of these people who says: "Oh yeah just go on with it. ... you'll be fine." and that's really - it's a bad thing to be like. and ... umm strengths? I think ... I'm very open-minded. umm I like to ... try new things and go to new places and ... see new cultures. so yeah that could be a ... umm strength I believe ... so

6. The ... - I think because I've a - I've previously taught ... English before, then it's nice to see ... a different group of people ... again, because like I said I've now taught many, but I've never actually taught ... students, so it'd be nice to see how ... they interact and how this - this system works ... with that, and ... I think ... what least interests me? I don't think anything ... doesn't interest me. umm ... no not ... - I can't think of anything really that ... would put me off. [laughs slightly] /Interviewer/ umm ... well least I think I would say ... the phonetical aspect ... of it. I've not ... unfortunately ... ever covered phonetics. therefore I ... don't really know a lot about it ... but umm ... like I said before the - I like to - I'd like to make my mark ... with ... putting ... pronunciation and getting people to realize that umm ... there's different types of ... the dialects, because obviously my accent's a lot different from ... other and that would be really nice. I ... like the idea that I could teach people ... a different way? than the way they are already taught. but it's still ... the correct way, so ... *that's a nice* ... yeah ... - I like to make my Scottish mark on [laughs]

7. Umm ... well ... it depends really. I think teaching ... can be ... both. ... it can be a bit of both. I like ... to ... work as a team ... to get ... help with ideas for things, and to think up lesson plans and so on and so forth, ... but as for the ... actual teaching ... part of it then I like ... - I have my own ... way of doing it, and my own ... way of thinking, so then it's a bit more individual. but I believe teaching's - you ... have a bit of both. you can't just be individual and you can't just work as a team. you need to have both parts. so

8. Umm ... if they're uncooperative then ... well ... it depends obviously a lot of the time on what kind of course they are doing, ... I like to think that if ... students are here ... to learn English then ... they WANT to learn it. therefore if ... - if they're uncooperative maybe they're having a bad day. so ... just say: "Look, ... as - you know I know you're having a bad day, but try a little bit." I like to encourage people: "You're doing good. ... there is no ... point in getting down about this, but ... you need to - to try." ... like I said [laughs slightly] I'm a bit unsympathetic, so [laughs] I think ... I'm not - I wouldn't just leave someone and go: "Oh yeah" ... but umm ... yeah I think most people who learn languages want to learn the language. so they tend to ... have ... - they tend to want to do it and have this ... kind of need ... to learn. and ... so yeah ... but definitely with university students I believe it will be different .... than with children [laughs] who really don't want to learn [laughs] so ... yeah

9. Criticism? umm it depends what kind of criticism I think. umm ... umm ... I think once again being a language student, ... I'm kind of used to criticism ... from ... trying to speak another language and someone saying: "Oh you're saying that wrong and you're saying that wrong." ... and I think I'm used to ... saying: "Oh, yeah, yeah" and ... I can ... handle it ok. but then again it depends again what situation. if someone criticizes my ... personal way of thinking, or my ... - I've had ... sometimes ... children in my classes who have criticized ... umm the way I have spoken, because they've not heard the Scottish ... accent before, ... and ... that's ... the ... - you have to ... then ... say to them: "Oh yeah well this is different and ..." that sometimes - it depends how badly they criticize I think. [laughs] so ... I don't know. ... I don't think I handle it too badly. I'm quite an easy going person so ... *not so bad.* [laughs]

10. Umm … not so much … public spea - like - obviously as a teacher, I've spoken in front of large classes before and … umm … and in my … classes at university, … and I'm really … quite happy to do it. it's not … - it doesn't frighten me, it doesn't … bother me at all. I'm quite happy to … - to … be in front of a group of people. *that's no problem.* but I've no … well … public - I've never taught a … lecture with - with one thousand well - one hundred people or anything, so nothing quite as grand as that. [laughs] but yeah I think I'd be - I'd be ok about it and … *hopefully everything … yeah should be fine.*
11. Hopefully yes. yeah. I believe I can. [laughs slightly]
12. Umm … I just wanted to ask about the phonetical side of it. because obviously I'm a bit … - I'm not sure about how that works. … how much - what would I really be expected to - to do? /Interviewer/ <oh ok, yeah, alright> of this yeah /interviewer/ pronunciation yeah /Interviewer/ so correctly yeah /Interviewer/ but … are the students taught the - are they taught the - the Queen's English then? /Interviewer/ so they'd be taught with things - ah see that's but /Interviewer/ <mhm, yeah, ok, oh yeah then, mhm, yeah> (that you deal) /Interviewer/ yeah … how big is … /Interviewer/ 100 people? /Interviewer/ wow /Interviewer/ <yeah, mhm> oh so they don't have to come. /Interviewer/ yeah /Interviewer/ of help - extra help for them. yeah yeah. /Interviewer/ to learn. /Interviewer/ yeah it's the best way I think to learn. … to have a native speaker in your class. /Interviewer/ it's much … much better than learning /Interviewer/ exactly /Interviewer/ no because they think just yeah /Interviewer/ yeah with students because they think if you have another … - if it's someone who is of … a position … that's higher, people are … a bit shyer and don't want to speak … yeah /Interviewer/ yeah I think yeah that should be fine. I'll brush up on my … Queen's English [laughs] /Interviewer/ but yeah I think … it's not so different though when it comes down to it really so … well that's fine. /Interviewer/ *so it wouldn't be … no problems.* thanks then. /Interviewer/ no I think that's about it. ( ) /Interviewer/ yeah no problem. [laughs]

I 32f

Sex: female
Age: 21
Origin: England, GB

1. Umm my name is 32[36], I come from England, I come from the north of England, but my father comes from the south of England, London. and my (mom) comes from the north. so ... my accent's probably slightly in between two. Umm ... I grew up completely in Yorkshire ... and ... I studied over in Yorkshire for my ... - for everything apart from my university studies. umm ... my university studies are in Wales, north Wales in Bangor, and I study ... a bachelor degree in German and modern Germany. so that entails all sorts of German history from ... film to media, to business, ... all sorts of how - how they all ... were introduced into the country, how they first started and what happens now, how they've changed and developed through the years really. [2 sec.] yeah

2. In Germany? well cause my degree is a German degree. it's compulsory... for us to study abroad. but ... I'd actually set my heart on coming to Passau really [laughs] umm ... I tried and tried and there was - there wasn't enough room and they wouldn't let me in and then in the end umm a very nice e-mail from my tutor actually ... allowed them to let me to study here for the whole year, because I'm only single honours ... umm ... but I just loved the idea of coming to Bavaria. I thought cause it's such ... - sort of stereotypical part of Germany, it's what I've - all the foreigners think of Germany but it's also that it's so far in the south. it's by the mountains, it's got great countryside and I'm very much a water person. I love being next to the water, it just makes you feel ... fresh and walking down the river every morning to lectures is something I really find ... is very good. invigorating. I think so ( ) [laughs]

3. As a tutor? umm I do think I'm a very outgoing and reliable person. umm ... a lot of people like to approach me, ask me questions I've done ... intercambio for the last semester ... and hopefully my intercambio

---

36 The number "32" is used here instead of the first name of the applicant.

is returning if not I've got a couple more people asking to do … inter-cambio with me, I was also part of the umm … Gmoa[37]-Aufsatz course last semester, which … involved umm … comp - compiling up data in interesting topics for people to write essays and helping them with how they write essays and having a … group conversation for an hour or so … just sort of - about … many different topics from a wide scope from politics to creative writing so … all kinds of vocabulary and things like that really, umm … ( ) I'm very punctual. I'm very organized. I'm a person that likes to get up nice and early and … come down at half past eight for these lectures [laughs] umm I also … - I'll - I just love … talking to people. I love … being … an active member within things I'm … I was a … active member in community theatre and things back at home. which meant … I had to perform in front of thousands and thousands of people at concert halls and I always help(ed) my own and spoke clearly and helped people. and also I just - I love help - I love be-ing in - involved in things, I think. I like to keep myself busy and things like that yeah

4. *Personal?* [laughs] *personal qualifications* umm I'm quite enthusias-tic. I feel quite strongly about a lot of different things. I love … - I like to catch up on the news and read the newspapers, especially in England at the moment with the umm … ( ) coming election, umm … but I like to be … - to - to form an opinion. by reading ev - every sort of source you can find on the topic so if it's big like … the new pope at the moment or something like that, I like to find out all the information … and I like to see both sides of an argument and if we're in like debating or if we're … helping with pronunciation it's always good to be able to keep a conversation flowing and … I sometimes feel that maybe I talk a little too much [laughs] but … hopefully it w - it would help people to feel … at ease around me and that … I can always help them with what they're saying and give them ideas as well.

5. *Strengths and weaknesses*…blimey … umm [2 sec.] I think that I … - I don't find it hard to talk to anybody. … I think that … whatever

---

37 "Gmoa" is the name of a social meeting place for students at the University of Passau.

... - whatever type of person it is, ... I can talk to them and ... get a positive ... sort of answer from them, a positive ... umm being and things from them. I think ... - with my jo - I work in a job as a waitress where I actually serve ... quite famous people. ... so I have to talk to these people as if they're just normal and not be like: "*oh my goodness* ... I'm with Gary Lineker" that sort of thing. but umm ... it's good to be able to find a level on which to talk to people, of - from anywhere, any stature, any history that they've got and so they feel comfortable and that they've got you know ... someone who ... is listening as well as ... taking in what they say and helping them. I feel that's a very good quality, a good strength ... in me. ... weaknesses umm [laughs] ... I think ... for the job ... a strong weakness is that I don't have ... a large linguistic background. I've ... not ... studied - studied linguistic in English since GCSE, ... but I have studied sort of linguistics in German. basic linguistics that you do within a language degree. sort of ... when we learn ... a grammatical term or how to say things in German, they always ... take it back to how you say it in English, how you form the sentence, how things are said in English, so you can then relate it to a German language. so that's - that's the sort of ... best knowledge I have. I haven't done a linguistics - linguistics isn't part of my degree. I can't do the phonetic alphabet or anything. [laughs]

6. *Most and least?* ... mostly I think it's the contact with students of German who are ... interested in learning English. because as English is becoming more and more ... a vital language to know ... in Europe and the European Union and the UN nationa - internationally as well. ... I find it very interesting that people ... want to speak the language but also like to speak the language ... properly with a good pronunciation and you know perfect speaking. and I always find when Germans ... say things to you and you're in a conversation you do sometimes find it hard to say: "actually you say it like this" and it'd be nice to be in a situation where you're meant to be doing that and people are genuinely interested. which had made me ... genuinely want to help them. I think. [3. sec] bu - w - umm ... bits of the job that I don't find int - I wouldn't like to do? ... umm ... I'm not sure really. I just - you get to have a go I think [laughs]

7. Umm [2 sec.] I think it depends on the work. ... if I'm preparing ... to ... teach. ... for example or preparing to do things ... where I - it's - it's of my own accord and I have to have for a personal mark, I like to do things on my own independently then I can ... organize my study time and ... work as much as I want, so if I'm preparing for - to do ... a presentation. I like to be able to think: "Right well I need to this presentation." so I'll work until I've got to a certain point, I'll set myself a goal. ... and then sometimes it's harder with people cause they'll say: "Oh can we not meet up until ..." you know ... "another day" and you ( ) of ... - is quite bad. but other times ... I find that teamwork is very advantageous because ... umm sometimes they give you ... input and opinions that you haven't thought about. which also helps you to increase your ... - your sort of - your level in which you're working at. ... so I sometimes think that for ... - for teamwork and team-presentations it's always very very important ... to have other ideas and not just - not to take control, sometimes to sit back and be more of a diplomat and ... say "what do you think?" "what do you think?" [laughs] I think it's - they both have their ... sort of ... pros and cons to ... doing both. I think it depends on the type of work mainly.

8. *When students are in a bad mood?* ... I try and lighten the mood. I think would be my - my ideal. [laughs slightly] I would sort of ... try and put some jokes in and make sure there's sort of ... a funny ... - a funny side to see of what's wrong with them. ... I would sort of joke around. if it was a serious problem, I would ... talk to them one on one and see if they'd like to talk to me about it first, not to force it out of them. but ... if they'd like to talk to me or ... if they'd like to talk to anybody else I would hopefully guide them to someone. or if they were just feeling ... down in the dumps and they just weren't really in the mood, I could try and ... brighten up their spirits with a few jokes and ... a few laughs.

9. *Criticism?* ... quite well. [laughs] I've got two brothers so [laughs] I think they - they generally like to criticize girls when they can't throw or - or [laughs] when they can't run quite as fast. so ... and norm - and normally ... if it's joke for criticism it [phone rings] oh yeah I can criticize back just as quickly. ... so ... would you like to take it? Or should we leave it? /Interviewer/ ok. I'd like - I like to criticize back ... or if -

155

if it's constructive criticism say ... in an essay or if I finish a speaking presentation and they say: "Well you could have done this b - but you could research this area" I would take that on board and I would ... for the next time I'll try and prove to them that the area which was criticized ... is much better. I don't think I ever take criticism [2 sec.] badly. I think it's ... I either... - it either helps me. or it kind of gets a rise out of me so I will criticize back just as badly. but I think I'd never get upset ... if someone criticized me.

10. Umm ... I love - I'll - I quite enjoy ... [laughs] - I'm not a big actor but umm with being in part of the youth community theatre for a very long time, I actually performed ... umm at the umm charity concerts. church Christmas concert at the umm world concert hall in Nottingham, which I was actually the host of the whole show so I - I g - I got to get a nice dress. [laughs] and I had to - I had to speak ... in front of two and a half thousand people so I was - ... I extremely ... you know I didn't stutter and I didn't ... - cause I had a cold at the time as well I wasn't stuttering and I wasn't sniffing, I was just - I kind of ... kept my posture and just thought: "At the end of that I can go to bed for a week." but ... otherwise I do like ... speaking in front of people. at first you get the adrenalin rush I think is a thing with me. I love that rush just before I go on ... and then when ... - when the crowd's appreciative of you it's much better. ... I've also done a little bit of radio work through the years of theatre as well and a bit of television, ... like interviews on television and interviews on radio about ... certain things I've been doing. ... but ... otherwise yeah ... it's been - it's - I love doing it. I really do. *I think.* [laughs slightly]

11. Yeah. (I) - hopefully, I am. yes. I think ... I would really like to start interacting with a lot more German students even if it is ... in the medium of English. I think ... it would be good for them to come ... and just be able to say if I needed help in German hopefully they would help me too, but ... I think just being able to help people is such a big ... - big important thing in my life is helping people out and ... just being there and if I can get to act a bit as well and [laughs slightly] prepare things properly that'd be brilliant.

12. *Do I have any questions?* umm what sort of material would you like? anything or? /Interviewer/ <yeah, oh well> texts or papers and things

yeah. ... oh brilliant. yeah ... *I - I think that's about it.* /Interviewer/ umm ... I don't think so. *I think th*at's about ... *everything.* [laughs] /Interviewer/ Oh you're welcome. thank you for offering me the job really. [laughs] give me the opportunity. [laughs]

I 33m

Sex: male
Age: 20
Origin: Dublin, Ireland

1. Okay. umm ... yeah umm ... I come from Ireland, ... umm I study in Dublin, but I live ... a little bit south maybe umm ... half an hour, ... in a smaller village, ... umm [2 sec.] I started a new CD two years ago, I'm doing ... commerce ... with German, the German is an arts degree, umm ... and then ... the year abroad, ... umm ... it is compulsory, it's part of the ... degree, ... so ... we had umm ... six different ... - six - six choices ... to go to and we have - had to make our own groups and then decide ... amongst ourselves ... where to go, so ... that was quite difficult for a while because ... actually a lot of people wanted to come to Passau, ... it sounded really good ... but ... it ended up the - the five of us. we - we were in ... the group we wanted and we got the place we wanted, so ... it worked out really well. /Interviewer/ *so yeah.*

2. In Germany? umm ... w - why I do German in college - like to start? / Interviewer/ yeah yeah well I mean ... umm ... umm yeah ... as I said it was part of the course to do German and you had to come here as part of the degree, but also I mean I wanted to ... - umm [2 sec.] I wanted to do an Erasmus year, ... anyway, so umm ... and Ge- Germany ... it sounded good I was here before a few years ago, ... and ... I had a really good time, so yeah, it's perfect.

3. Umm ... /Interviewer/ oh yeah umm yeah I've umm ... - I've ... - I've done some tutor work before, ... umm in secondary school, ... not umm ... - not in German, but for other stuff, so I - it's ... - I've ... t - ... helped people before, I've taught some people before, ... umm ... it's ... - it was umm it worked out yeah - it worked out very well. umm I could get ... the point across and you just don't umm - you need some patience obviously, ... *if* it's a strange subject or whatever ... that's fine. ... *(like) ... just patience and I can ... talk to people no problem. ... I can deal with it.*

4. As in ... [3 sec.] wi - umm personal qual [2 sec.] - how do you mean? /Interviewer/ oh oh personal yeah character - sorry! okay okay ( )

meant diplomas or something. umm ... well I - I was like meeting with new people, ... I'm ... quite p - patient with them, ... I mean there's no problem like if ... - is - umm I mean I had ... - I had difficulties with German at the start ... umm still do, [laughs slightly] well ... a bit. so umm ... when people try to help the teachers you can appreciate it can be difficult, so there is no problem with that, umm ... I've quite ... a broad range of interests, so we can talk about anything, ... there's no problem there, umm [2 sec.] and [2 sec.] yeah I think ... - I think I'm ... easy enough to get along with [laughs slightly] so ... it should be okay ... *yeah.*

5. As a tutor? or ... /Interviewer/ in general? umm ... weaknesses [2 sec.] umm [3 sec.] sometimes yeah I can - I get angry with myself sometimes, when I - when I can't [2 sec.] - for example with the German some-times, ... over here you think ... - you think you're - you're you know you learn more and more every day, ... so you think you're doing fine, but then ... maybe somebody is talking in German and you don't un-der - understand, ... and all of a sudden you think: ... "Damn this is really not so good." but then maybe you hear "Oh they are speaking in a niederbayerisch accent." or so [laughs slightly] it's no problem there. I can get kind of annoyed of myself. I should ... have a bit more pa-tience maybe ... with myself. umm [2 sec.] umm ... *other weaknesses?* [3 sec.] I can't think of any *(you'd have to ask)* somebody else, one of my friends. [laughs] ( ) umm ... strengths oh yeah as I said ... I mean ... for this just ... patience, I can ... interest in a lot of things, umm ... so I can ... - easy to ... talk to people, ... umm and I like to - *it's* ... interesting meeting with ... n - people you know, umm obviously here there is l - loads of ... - loads of foreign students, so there's umm ... a huge amount of people we've gotten to know, ... have great time with, so ... and the - the more the better ... you know, ... so ... yeah and also - also - like - I mean I just ... in general like ... umm ... umm ... we had a - a ... - kind of a tutor in secondary school, and umm ... a few of them ... - l - like - the kind of like this, the ... ones a few years older and they helped us with ... - with the German, so I - I'd like to ... help people with English then as well, cause I know it - it ... - I can understand it can be difficult ( ) a language and pronunciation as well can be tricky so, umm ... yeah I like ... he - helping people ... *learn.*

159

6. Umm [2 sec.] the most umm [2 sec.] the chance to talk some English, [laughs] so I - I know that I'm ... not making mistakes maybe [laughs slightly] ... or hopefully, umm ... umm as I say yeah the - the chance to meet some people ... umm to meet people and [2 sec.] yeah because I - I mean ... - to be honest I mean ... s - some - a little money would help ... obviously as well, umm ... Pa - Passau is cool it's not too expensive but just ... umm ... umm ... *I wouldn't have to ask for so much from my parents (for) whatever, so ... that too*, but ( ) also - also we don't have ... an awful lot of hours ... in our timetable, ... so umm [2 sec.] umm we'll be in the university a little more and just be around and not just ... lazing around all the time ... you know /Interviewer/ and then [2 sec.] was it both of them? /Interviewer/ most and least? ... *(what)* did I say? /Interviewer/ oh oh the least yeah yeah. the least ... umm ... the only thing I can think of ... umm [2 sec.] maybe if ... sometimes when you know you do some trips away or something maybe if something comes up that might clash with the class ... I don't know ... but I mean that can ... - *it's not a huge thing.* umm ... can you - do you know can you do ... if there's four classes of 45 minutes can you do two on the same day or? /Interviewer/ oh you can? well that's perfect. that should be fine ... *cool.* I was just thinking maybe if you had to do four separate ... evenings, then that's four evenings you can't ... /Interviewer/ ( )

7. Umm [4 sec.] as in for something like this or in general? /Interviewer/ umm [3 sec.] well in school - in school ... that's interesting yeah - in school that was all independent, for ( ) so that was fine, umm ... I kind of liked the fact you know it was up to you, ... what you did, you weren't depending on people, and people didn't depend on you, ... so ... you didn't feel ... like you were to ask other people to do work and then you didn't feel like ... if you took a day off maybe you were letting other people down, but then when I got to college a lot more of it was project work and team work, ... and umm ... it helps you know when ... you'd some ... projects to do and ... - quite tough but - ... you know if you're four people and ... the idea is just ... umm like a snowball effect, once you start getting a few ideas a lot of it comes together, and then also ... obviously you don't - you don't ... umm ... you don't want to work in a group with people who just ... don't care

at all cause I mean then it's hard ... ( ) everybody. but even - even in a good group ... there'll always be - certain differences arise, but ... y - you learn how to kind of - ... you learn how to compromise and that so and ... working in groups is interesting as well. I think they call it group dynamics. [laughs slightly] but I know that so umm ... I know that in s - in s - in some ways working independently is grand and in other ways ... team work is also fun. ... so they both have *advantages and disadvantages.*

8. Right. /Interviewer/ umm ... capital punishment ( ) [laughs] no umm umm [4 sec.] probably [2 sec.] umm ( ) [3 sec.] probably ex - explain to them how - ... I mean sometimes ... when I've been tutored as well or - or in class you feel the same. everyone feels the same sometimes. I'd just [3 sec.] say to them ... umm [2 sec.] like "I - I know how you feel, it - it can be tough and that but just ... - just try your best and just get - come through it and then afterwards you can ... go and relax and sleep or just get some food or whatever", also then if umm ... - if ... you notice they were particularly tired or something or - or they don't cooperative, just not - not to do ... too much, just ... you know not to ... (load off on work) or whatever because then ... there's no point. and then – (like another times if) they seem particularly ... en- thusiastic or whatever you can do a little more, because they're more willing, they're more receptive. so yeah if - if they are a bit umm ( ) just try not to umm [2 sec.] - try just ... - talk to them and try to say: "Yeah I know how you feel - I mean I've - we've all been there ... but you just ... try and get through it" and then ... as well as just not to ... do too much ( )

9. Criticism? umm ... if I - if I think it's umm - I'm always open to con- structive criticism, I mean nobody's perfect, so if - if - if people ... make a point about something that I can improve on, then g - great, like that's - that's fine. ... umm ... i - if - if the criticism isn't fair I - I'll argue. I - I can't help enough argue I just ... if - if I feel the criticism isn't fair, it's - I don't - I don't like that. and I - I'd never [2 sec.] - (*well*) if I was to criticise other people I'd always - I'd never do it like ... - think it through and just make sure you are right because I know - I know how umm ... - unfair criticism really annoys me so I ... hate ... ha - I'd hate to think I'd be doing it to somebody else, ... but then constructive

criticism is good I think. umm ... some of my teachers like were real - they were ... quite like that. and I - I know some people don't like it. I mean sometimes they - they might seem to shout or something and some people ... don't take that well, but I mean if - if they make sense then ... I realize it's nothing personal, it's just something - they are really trying to help you, ... so that's constructive criticism. it's grand ... perfect). but ... if I think it's unfair I'll argue. [laughs slightly] *yeah.* (*The next one.*) [directed towards the interviewer, meaning "ask the next question"]

10. Umm ... public speaking ... in - in college when you do umm ... your - your umm ... midterm-work like a presentation, ... s - sorry yeah ... in school there's not - there isn't much ... umm ... you know it's like exams - written exams and stuff (your hand up). but in college there's a lot of oral ... tests so ... you do your presentation and obviously there is marks for the content, ... but then also it's for your presentation, how you connect with the class and ... how you kept their interest, umm ... the - the first [2 sec.] - I've - I've never had a problem really talking in public ... to - to a large group of people. ... (Having) said that ... umm ... after ... like college - after two years (I've been) doing stuff, ... stuff does prove just ... your tone of voice, looking ... around and ... I don't know maybe hand gestures or whatever, but yeah I've no - no problem ... speaking ... in public or to people.

11. Yeah definitely. *yeah sure.*

12. Umm [2 sec.] no. ... oh umm [3 sec.] is it - is it like pronunciation as in ... umm ... - is it just pronunciation? or ...? /Interviewer/ <okay, oh yeah> pronunciation yeah of course ... yeah ... sure ... of course yeah no problem. definitely. /Interviewer/ all right. /Interviewer/ no problem.

I 34f

Sex: female
Age: 21
Origin: Salisbury, GB

1. [laughs slightly] well I'm from Salisbury which is south ... west England central west umm and I study in Cardiff which is actually in Wales not England, umm I've just finished my second year in Cardiff. ... studying ... English literature and German ... umm ... which ... I really enjoy, I didn't mean to go to university and study German it was just ... - I ... did it in my first year and enjoyed it. so *umm* ... I'm really grateful though for the opportunity to stay here for a year which ... is a bit like a gap year at the moment [laughs] more fun than studying but it's good umm [2 sec.] I don't - what should I say about myself? like ... I'm ... f - from a small ... city. ... like Passau, ... umm with the same number of inhabitants and ... a beautiful cathedral and ... old architecture it's very nice ... umm ... [laughs slightly] I live there with my family but ... in Cardiff I obviously live with ... my friends, ... which I miss at the moment but that's good. [laughs slightly] it's nice

2. Umm well my mum ... - I - ... my mum umm spoke German she ... worked here as a nurse. ... twenty years ago or so. so ... that was why I originally chose to study German ... at school. and then I actually gave it up. but took it up back again at university. just ... umm ... for fun really and then I enjoyed it. so I decided to carry on with it. especially ... umm in England we are so f-... lazy. I've had to say faul [laughs] yeah we're so lazy cause everyone speaks English. so actually ... I think it gives ... my English literature degree ... something extra. by having a language. ... - it - when - yeah - on the job market. hopefully.

3. Umm ... well ... for - umm communication I've worked ... as a - I took a year out between school and ... university where I worked as a dive master, which umm - teaching scuba diving. so ... I had to work with people from ... all different nationalities. it was in Australia. so everyone went there to dive. so I think that made - umm ... in that situation communication was very important like ... they had to understand what I was telling them and I ... had to make sure they understood

what I was saying cause ... it would have been dangerous otherwise. so that helped. and then I've - I - I've worked ... umm in bars since 18, so communicating and working with people ... has never been a problem. and it's something I actually enjoy. [laughs slightly]

4. Umm ... I'm ... very ... easy to talk to ... and open ... and ... umm ... I enjoy talking. and learning things about people ... and talking to people. *so* [laughs slightly]

5. [laughs] umm [2 sec.] my strengths [2 sec.] umm ... I hate questions like that! [laughs] I'm honest ... I guess [laughs slightly] I'm ... - I'm very friendly. ... and ... umm [2 sec.] I'm ... motivated ... when I find something stimulating, ... and I'm interested in lots of different things. I'm very tolerant of people, ... my weaknesses? ... umm [2 sec.] I can be opinionated, [laughs] and a bit loud at times [laughs slightly] I guess ... I think that's [laughs] - there's probably other ones [laughs] but ... yeah

6. Umm [2 sec.] *aspects* [2 sec.] - just ... - I think it'd be ... interesting ... at the moment umm because I don't have to ... really ... take any exams here. the only work I have to do is for my home university. there's umm ... a slight lack of structure to my day, so ... that aspect of like - umm it's also quite nice to have - to be doing other things and meeting new people. because I've already - I've made a group of friends here. I'm - I think we become quite anti-social once you're comfortable. so ... that will be interesting. umm [3 sec.] umm interesting me least? there's nothing really that doesn't interest me, ... as long as it's not at seven in the morning! [laughs]

7. Umm [2 sec.] it depends. I - I quite like - I'm quite independent person. so I do like to work ... mostly independently. but then [3 sec.] like - umm for example going to lectures at the moment I really enjoy going with a person especially because they're in German so ... you can sit there and just be like ... what was that? [laughs] and I like to share that experience with someone. rather than on your own. [laughs slightly]

8. Umm ... ideally I like to ignore people's moods. [laughs] a mood like that that's not ... really umm ... positive. if - if they were in a bad mood for a reason I could ask why. ... but if it's just umm [2 sec.] something pri - I don't know that they don't want to share obviously

then ... I wouldn't let that get in the way. I'd just be ... extra merry. [laughs] make up for it. [laughs slightly]

9. Umm ... I - I hope well. ... it depends, I suppose, what they are criticising. [laughs slightly] constructively I'd like to think. [laughs slightly]

10. Umm ... in Eng - I found I'll - enjoy speaking in public in English. I'll - I umm ... - in school I did lots of ... drama and ... - and singing. I've done a lot of music. I play ... the cello and the piano and I sing. so performing I really enjoy. but then I found I was in ... Wildbad Kreuth ... two weeks ago for the s ... - seminars. and we had to talk - do a little talk about our country in German. ... and I can`t do public speaking in German [laughs slightly] I found. I think I'd have to be a bit more confident but ... my head just goes empty. so [laughs slightly]

11. I'd like to know ... probably more about it cause I just have the e-mail. but ... I can handle anything generally. I'm confident of that. [laughs]

12. Umm like about the job. so ... w - what would the ... 45 minute classes involve? like ... not classes ( ) ... *meetings* /Interviewer/ <mhm> then do - and do I ... like ... do I structure the classes or you tell me? or not classes, groups - like do I just structure the conversation or? /Interviewer/ <right> something like stimulus *and* /Interviewer/ how many people would *be in a ... group?* /Interviewer/ *that's scary.* ( ) *interesting.* [laughs] and would ... - how do you decide when the ... groups would be? like what time? /Interviewer/ that depends. mhm. /Interviewer/ <right, mhm, laughs slightly> *I think that's it* /Interviewer/ yeah. /Interviewer/ [laughs slightly] that's okay

I 35m

Sex: male
Age: 21
Origin: Seattle, WA, USA

1. Umm ... my name it 35[38], I come from ... umm Washington State, ... umm ... close to Seattle, but not exactly, umm ... in the United States I study government ... and politic and ... philosophy ... and ... I've been studying German for ... about two years, ... and umm [4 sec.] *I don't know what else I should say.* [laughs slightly]

2. Umm ... my family ... is actually German. umm ... my grandparents on both of my parents' side came from Germany. and so ... everybody in my family can speak a little bit of German ... I've heard lots of stories about ... back when ... people of my family would still live in Germany or come back to visit family. ... so it's always been ... - been ... so exciting ... and something so far away and amazing for me. and then I ... finally got this opportunity ... when I was at university, so I ... just had to jump on.

3. Umm ... well I've studied ... English ... a lot. I've taken many ... college English courses and writing courses and ... other things like that. so I believe that my ... - my **English** is certainly professional. ... *I mean* I'm a native English speaker. ... and ... also I have worked umm tutoring people and - both younger than I and older than I and teaching classes and things like that before. so I think I have at least some sort of experience. so ... that should definitely help.

4. Umm ... I think I'm very patient ... and ... very relaxed and so I can ... umm ... take my time and understand people's problems and tell where - where they may be having ... umm misunderstandings and kind of go through this ... slowly with them. ... I think that's probably one of the most important characteristics of a - a ... teacher or tutors, to be patient with their students.

5. Umm ... okay my strengths I think I am ... very patient and ... - and understanding and I can - ... I can help people ... umm ... build their - their language skills through ... communication and through writing

---

38 The number "35" is used here instead of the first name of the applicant.

and whatever else. ... and ... my weaknesses maybe I'd probably be too lenient with students, if they're speaking too much German in class or whatever I would ... probably let that slide or ... - or not be too ... - too strict. ... but ... that's probably the most serious. [laughs slightly]

6. Umm [3 sec.] it kind of - I guess it would kind of depend. umm ... in a situation like this ... then I - umm ... it would ... maybe be better to work with one other person, ... because ... then we can kind of build off of each other. and - ... and ... both come up with ideas to help ... (the other) students (be) learning and ... - and practicing, ... but if it's ... in a different situation like in some sort of ... project where you have to ... umm create some sort of presentation or ... - or some sort of product then I'd probably rather work alone.

7. Umm ... I think it would be ... great to umm ... first of all meet other German students, cause since I am an Erasmus student here most of the people that I have met are other Erasmus students form different countries. so it would definitely be nice to meet ... umm lots of German people and ... - and I think it would also help build my German, ... because then ... after class we can speak in German or something like that. ... and umm [3 sec.] *umm* ... and also I think it will help umm ... my understanding of German and English both because if I have to explain something then ... - then I would understand it myself better. ... umm [2 sec.] and I guess I don't really know what I would ... umm least looking forward to, because I'm not exactly sure what is gonna happen. so ... - *so I don't really know if I can answer that.*

8. Umm ... if - I guess if somebody is in a bad mood and just ... doesn't wanna be there, then ... you know I guess ... what would be ... probably the easiest is either ... tell them to ... relax and ... *yeah umm* participate or ... you know just do something else. ... either that or if they really don't want to participate then I would probably say you're free to leave ... and come back when you're ... in a better mood and more ... - more excited about ... doing whatever it is that we are doing.

9. Umm ... I'm - I've h - I think I would handle it very well you know it's - I take it as umm ... - as ... - as a learning tool you know. if somebody tells me you know "you're doing this wrong and this wrong and this wrong" then those are the things that I need to work on. and

the things that I need to change … and just to make myself better, … teaching better or my instruction better or … - or … anything.

10. Mhm I have umm been doing speech and debate competitions … for … five or six years, … so I have … had to give many speeches in front of class rooms and in front of auditoriums and … - and so. … I - I don't think I would really have any … umm fear *of that or anything.*

11. Certainly. I mean I … - my English is - is … probably … as good or better than anybody else and … I've … done lots of public speaking and lots of tutoring before and … - and … I can't think of any reason why I would have any problems.

12. Umm … I don't think so. maybe about … the structure, about … what - what exactly happens. how often we meet or … /Interviewer/ <mhm, okay> okay and how many people ( )?… /Interviewer/ okay. … umm [2 sec.] and when … would the classes be meeting? mornings or afternoons? or? /Interviewer/ <okay, mhm> okay. … and how much … English experience would these student have had …? /Interviewer/ <mhm, okay, yeah> I think that's all the questions I have. /Interviewer/ well certainly.

I 36m

Sex: male
Age: 20
Origin: Dublin, Ireland

1. Okay umm well my name is 36[39] and I come from Ireland and live in the main city centre ... the ... capital, which is Dublin, umm ... I'm over here in Passau for the year with four other guys ( ) we're studying BWL, so we've done Commerce and German at home in UCD that's our university over there, and so we do two years there and then we have to do a year abroad and then we go back for our final year, so we all wanted to go travel together so we decided to choose Passau, so ... we've been here a month now and we haven't gone to - we're just getting into the swing of things with class and all but umm ... it's going well, and ... - and ... what else? ... umm ... ( ) ... umm [2 sec.] umm ... I like to play sports ... I ... like to read a bit as well umm ... generally like to just hang out with people and socialize a lot. and ... I like to travel as well so that was - doing this course obviously appealed to me cause I got to go away for a year, ... and I'd only ever been to Germany once before but only for three or four days, so it's good to ... use my - it's good to use my language over here, ... and [3 sec.] there's ... a bit of family over there [laughs slightly] I've got two sisters, a mum and a dad and they're coming over to visit me on Thursday, ... so I'm looking forward to showing them everything in Passau so ... I have to do a bit of research first for a few days see where everything is, [laughs slightly] umm [3 sec.] that's ( ) [laughs slightly]

2. Umm ... it was probably ... umm when I was around twelve or ... when I was - went into first year. when I was twelve in secondary school ... you had to do two languages so I studied French and German, ... and ... the German teacher was really interesting and really - he made the subject very ... easy and really appealing to ... everybody in the class, ... so when I was around fifteen or sixteen I had to choose between ... French and German, and I chose German cause I - I was - I thought I was a bit better at it and I also enjoyed it

---

39 The number "36" is used here instead of the first name of the applicant.

a lot more, ... so I think the teacher definitely had a big influence on me. umm ... and I – I've been pretty happy with - with my choice. well let's see the grammar is a bit difficult but umm ... it's going well so far and then ... so I decided to ... - when I left school I ... really enjoyed the German it was one of my best subjects so ... I wanted to do a business course so I said I wanted to keep my language, so there was a course in college that offered me to do both so ... that was very handy so I took that course and I'm really happy with it. ... yeah so cause I know some people are doing the same course as me but ... they don't do a language and it's just a lot of the same stuff it's only business, so it's good to have business and then you're going into a different class with different people and you're doing German so ... I'm ... pretty happy with *it*. [laughs slightly] yeah.

3. Umm [3 sec.] I don't know well I ... consider myself quite an outgoing person. I love to play sport and umm ... I've ... done summer camps where I'd be coaching kids and all so. well obviously I'll be dealing with people a lot older but I'm - I'm used to dealing with people, ... and ... so I - like I ... love to communicate *with people* - I get on well with people so ... I think definitely through ... sport I will obviously get - I was coaching a team so they're round ten or eleven, ... so that was quite handy, so you obviously you get to deal - obviously they're gonna have problems and they'd be ... umm moaning sometimes but ... you got to - you get a ... lot of experience handling ... people like that. so that's obviously gonna help a lot umm and ... just from being in small classes myself in - in college maybe being in tutorials or classes, you know how the class operates so ... you'd know what - what you're expected to do and what's required from yourself.

4. (That's) [laughs slightly] umm isn't that kind of the same as the last question or? /Interviewer/ umm ... personal qual - umm [2 sec.] well obviously I speak English so [laughs slightly] that's gonna help. umm [3 sec.] *right* I – don't know if the - I can't really [3 sec.] sorry I'm just trying to think, it just seems similar to the other question umm [2 sec.] I don't know I just think I'm *an* easy enough person to talk to. so I'm ... sure I get on all right with everybody. ... and [2 sec.] - and if they've - ever have any problems I think I'd be an easy enough person to approach so ... I don't think there'd be any problems there

5. Umm [3 sec.] I'd say strengths umm I ... consider myself kind of ... umm a leader person that umm ... I think that I ... can set a good example ... and ... umm weaknesses ... umm sorry [laughs slightly] - umm I suppose umm [4sec.] - I umm ... sorry I'm trying to think [laughs] umm [2 sec.] well another str - strength would be kind of outgoing and ... I like to talk and all. but umm weaknesses? umm ... I suppose [3 sec.] umm ... [laughs slightly] I'm so sorry ( ) not really sure ... can't really think umm [2 sec.] I suppose umm [5 sec.] I don't know I like - I don't know well it can be a strength and a weakness. I kind of - if something I'm not happy with I'll say it ... so sometimes I can get you in a bit of trouble but on the other side I think it's good to be able to express your opinion ... and see if there's a problem but ... other times it can maybe ... - people mightn't be happier (with) what you say but umm ... that might be considered a weakness. but ... I think it's kind of a strength as well. [laughs slightly] umm [2 sec.] okay. [laughs slightly]

6. Umm [2 sec.] so i-... it would be interesting getting ... - like I know it - it's ... - for me it's good going over to learn a new language so it'll be good - in - interesting ... for me to be the one that has ... all the answers [laughs slightly] where I'll be ... my language will be ... good and I won't be struggling all the time like with my German but umm ... I think I'd be - I'm looking forward to see ... how German people learn English, like what they'll be like and it'll be good talk - like it'll only be a small group ... so you get to know the people pretty well ... and then that'll be good cause I get to know some more German people and maybe when I'm out ... not working you can ... socialize with them as well and maybe ... I can speak a bit of German to them as well so that would be ... - that'd be quite a ... - a good part of the course. umm [3 sec.] I don't think there's that many bad things about it. I think it's - I think it's a good idea ... so

7. Umm ... well I - I like to play ... umm football and rugby so I kind of like - sportswise I like to play in a team I think a team environment is very good. but then again I'm - I'm also capable of umm looking after myself and ... I don't mind if I'm ... thrown in somewhere ... in the deep end and I'm – I have I have to do the thing myself, ... that doesn't really bother me. umm ... so I'd be comfortable with either. I - like ... there's - there's positives and ... negatives of both ... both sides.

8. Umm ... I always think it's very im - like even when I'm in ... - at home in college or whenever I'm doing a presentation, I like to be - a lot of people just go up there and ... they just talk and ... they'd be very boring and they'd nearly put themselves to sleep so ... I'd like to be quite lively ... and ... I'd just like to make ... the classes enjoyable as - and as enthusiastic as possible, ... so I'd like to chan... - like I wouldn't ... like to be just ... umm monotonous and the same thing all the time. I'd like to do different things and ... maybe interact with them as much as possible and ... if I see there's something wrong like umm ... - you know I'll just ask them and ... yeah I - I - I wouldn't let anybody just ... out on their own and not feel like they're not part of class or anything.

9. Umm ... I think I can take criticism pretty well cause ... as I ...umm ... I think it takes a lot for a person to say something if they think that something is wrong. ... and obviously if they feel (about it) and if then somebody else feels as well the - there obviously is something wrong. so I def - I ... take it on the chin and accept it.

10. Umm ... yeah umm ... in col ... - in school I ... was on a German [laughs slightly] debating team for a while and ... umm in college we always have to make presentations in front of ... 50 people or even in small groups so ... I'm not really that fazed by (that). it's okay. ... *it doesn't bother me.* [laughs slightly] so it'll be all right.

11. Yeah I'd say it'd be fine.

12. Umm ... no. just how - I heard it's ... - it was a ... - four hours a week ... or? /Interviewer/ yeah. and ... think (having to) choose your hours or ... how does it work or? /Interviewer/ <mhm, okay> umm ... yeah so umm would you be able - if it's ... 45 minutes each time ... - so would you be able to maybe do ... 45 and then 45 straight afterwards? /Interviewer/ yeah? so just be at it and maybe do them in two blocks of two. /Interviewer/ <right, okay> *no that (was fun.)* /Interviewer/ okay no problem.

I 37f

Sex: female
Age: 20
Origin: Shipley, Bradford, West Yorkshire, GB

1. Yeah I come from a town called Shipley in West Yorkshire like ( ), umm
   it ... lies in the city of Bradford. it's very close to the boarder of Leeds
   so it's a lot bigger than Passau. I go to university in Kingston upon Hull
   ... and ... I've been studying ... law with German law and language for
   two years, but my actual study in Hull ... is based on ... English law
   ... and German language. it's a qualifying law degree in ... the English
   sense. and then the German law part comes in here when I bring ... -
   when I - when I umm ... have my year abroad in ... Germany ... so I
   chose to come to Passau. I could have gone to ... Erlangen, Osnabrück
   ... or Düsseldorf ... as well [2 sec.] mhm. ... umm ... last year at the
   university I took part in ... a kind of a teacher - tea - umm teacher training project as well. I was quite interested when I got your e-mail. umm
   and it was from - by ... the teacher training organization in England and
   they're piloting projects ... in cities where ... umm not so many young
   people are going on into ... higher education in England. and ... they
   pick students from university to go into local secondary schools umm
   I actually went into a sixth form college. and that - it was the first year
   that a sixth form college participated. ... and I taught ... *what's* - umm
   ... some classes and participated ... in classes in ... law, German, ...
   history, ... art [2 sec.] and I did something called personal development
   which is about filling in applications ( ) applications for university.

2. Well I studied German. ... GCSE, ... I enjoyed doing them. *I didn't* -
   well I got a good grade ... and ... took it on to A-Level. ... I'd always
   wanted to study law ... and I really enjoyed doing A-Level German,
   ... and so I looked at courses where I could combine ... German ...
   with law ... and I thought it would be ... a good idea because ... law
   is ... more and more competitive, ... to have a language as well is just
   ... - is - well it's really rewarding to be able to speak another language
   with other people, it's an excellent experience having the opportunity
   to live abroad for a year. and it's - it's good for - when you're to ... get
   a job - enhancing your career ... umm prospects ... really.

3. My qual - well ... the umm ... - project I took part in in Hull obviously. ... that was really good. I actually ... took - I actually took a few ... lessons in - in law and I prepared them and ... stood on the boar- [laughs slightly] in front of the board and wrote on the board and ... talked to the students and helped them. ... umm ... I think that - that qualifies me quite ... well in that aspect.

4. Umm ... well you've got to be able to communicate with people, talk clearly, be patient with them, I understand myself because I've learned German and it can be quite frustrating learning another language. and you can't expect people to ... know straight away. you just got to ... help and guide and ... - with the language.

5. Umm [11 sec.] in what kind of - oh in - in the teaching aspect. ... my strengths ... I'd say I'm ... - I'm quite ... umm able to communicate with people. I'm not shy when it comes to talking to people, getting to know other people, I'm not bothered about standing up in front of the class, ... umm ... and conducting a lesson. I'm not shy or embarrassed in that kind of aspect. Weaknesses [3 sec.] it's very hard picking out weaknesses ( ) ... *yourself isn't it?* umm [5 sec.] umm [7 sec.] *I'd have to think about it* [16 sec.]. I'm really not sure what I'd say ... when it comes to teaching. [4 sec.] weaknesses I'd have. ... I found that I dealt quite well with it when I took this project in Hull when I was - I was quite able to umm ... to do it. so ... it's quite a hard question. [laughs slightly]

6. Umm ... most is ... being able to ... help other people with their language. ... umm ( ) well ... because I learn German, it's nice when people help me ... umm [4 sec.] interests me LEAST about the job? [2 sec.] well ... I wouldn't be here if it didn't interest me so [laughs] I can't really say that.

7. Both. ... it really doesn't bother ... umm me I - I like working ... individually one to one with people and in a group.

8. *I'd be as* ... HAPPY as possible and try and encourage them to ... take part. I'd probably do ... a group activity and ... try and lighten their mood a bit.

9. Constructive criticism I think is very valuable. if ... people don't tell you where you're going wrong then you can't better yourself, you can't improve what you're doing wrong.

10. *Yeah I've done this classroom project. umm … I umm I've* never been afraid to … stand up in a classroom *and say "well this is what I think."*
11. *Yeah. … yeah very.*
12. Umm [6 sec.] what kind of … level would you be teaching in - in - in classes? /Interviewer/ <yeah, mhm> /Interviewer/ so it'd be kind of just having a conversation about what they've been doing during the week? [2 sec.] or? /Interviewer/ <mhm, yes> that's really good. there's nothing like that in England available to us so … yeah /Interviewer/ and … it would be meeting four times a week with the students? /Interviewer/ <mhm> so how many … English *people are you looking for then?* /Interviewer/ <really?> yeah four hours a week. /Interviewer/ <mhm, yeah> *yeah I think that was everything.* /Interviewer/ *welcome.*

I 38m

Sex: male
Age: 20
Origin: Brighton, GB

1. Umm ... my name is 38[40] I come from Brighton in England, born and
    bred there ... umm I study in Cardiff University in Wales, ... I study
    law and German. ... so I'm here now - over here now doing umm a
    law course. ... obviously for a year. ... and umm ... what else would
    you like to know? [laughs slightly] /Interviewer/ [laughs]

2. Umm at school I - I was - umm I learned - I've been learning German
    since I was ... umm ... thirteen years old in school. ... and umm it's
    umm - it had always been my ... favourite subject. so ... to carry it
    on at university was more of a natural ... umm ... persuasion than
    choice. so umm I did umm that and as well I was quite interested
    in ... law in the first place so ... law and German kind of married
    them so

3. As a tutor? ... umm ... well [2 sec.] perhaps not qualifications. I've
    done all my A-levels and ... my GCSEs, got very good grades in all
    of them. ... as well. umm ... perhaps more of my experience (would)
    be ... a lot more useful to this particular job. ... because I was a - a
    language tutor in a language school for ... umm well we had a lot of
    German students there as well. and I was teaching them more ... spe-
    cific language like ... for sciences, GCSEs and so on. ... so umm I think
    that would be a lot more useful than ... any qualifications I could give
    you at this point. [short interruption] so umm ... umm ... well umm
    ... obviously because of my umm - I've been trying to get experience
    in this ... kind of field for a long time. so that's how I got the job in
    the first place at the language school in Brighton. and umm ... beca -
    bec - I've been ... looking for this kind of experience because after
    university I plan to go into ... teaching. ... and eventually to set up my
    own school. I'm not sure whether a language school or umm ... umm
    just a normal school but umm

---

40 The number "38" is used here instead of the first name of the applicant.

4. Personal. I consider myself a very friendly person. I'd hope other people would say the same. umm ... friendly person. ... and I ... don't take myself too seriously so ... there's always that side of me. umm ... I'm very patient with people. ... especially people that are trying to learn new things. ... umm and umm ... obvi - I'm a ... great lover of languages so [2 sec.] I suppose that would play in my favour as well. [laughs slightly]

5. Generally? ... strengths umm ... strengths when I really want to do something I will do it and I'll stay with it till the end. umm ... such as my - my studies. umm ... I've had ... a nu - number of ... umm times where I could have just dropped out quite easily ... and ... be done with the work because it just wasn't what I wanted to do at that particular time but I've stayed with it and I'm very happy that I have. umm [3 sec.] weaknesses? [7 sec.] I know it sounds really bad but I - I can't think of anything that comes to ... - I'm sure there are. ... but umm [4 sec.] yeah perhaps I'm not modest enough. [laughs]

6. This tutori - this tutor job? well obviously it's umm - it interests me ... in-wholly cause this is the field I want to go into ... when I leave university. umm ... apart from that I just - I - I love the feeling of teaching people. ... umm I - I ... learned that I did when I was working as a tutor in this language school. it was very good to see umm ... the ideas that I ... umm put across to people come out in their thinking as well. ... and umm ... yeah ... it stre - you see - you - you - you do see the ... - the language pro-gressing with them as well. and certain words that you taught them and certain phrases that you taught them, when they come out then [2 sec.] umm it - it's - it's very nice to ... be able to see that coming out.

7. It really depends what kind of job it is. umm ... I'd say with more the - more academic side I'm - I'm much more independent worker. umm I can do my own work and be very ... umm ... umm good with my timing and ... good with the time that I do ... put towards it. umm ... when ... things do call for things to be ... umm done in a team I - I can also do that very ... easily it's ... umm not a problem for me. I get on with - well with people ... I umm haven't got a ... overbearing person-ality so umm [laughs slightly] it's not that I - I speal - steal the spotlight or anything it's umm yeah

8. [7 sec.] well it's umm ... *I* - I suppose it really does depend what's ... causing the bad mood but umm [2 sec.] generally I'd say try and do

something a little more stimulating, a little more fun. but still … obviously try and learn because … I know that - when I … learn something new there's a great … deal of satisfac - satisfaction that comes through that and … if you solve the problem that you haven't been able to … solve beforehand then obviously that's a great feeling as well so … perhaps something that would allow them to … experience that kind of feeling, would bump their mood up as well. … umm … yeah so just … umm bring it down a level … so it's not so formal and a little bit more fun … and umm [2 sec.] o - otherwise just see yeah [laughs slightly]

9. You can't really get ahead without any criticism … can you? I mean … as - as long as it's constructive I'm very happy to get criticism cause it will help me you … - umm [3 sec.] umm … o - overcome my mistakes and … - and better my - better myself than I have done before.

10. Umm yeah I mean … at my school it was always - the public speaking was always a big part of the umm - … umm the school curriculum. I was umm - I've done a number of them school assemblies umm - presentations before school assemblies. umm appearing in public has never been that much of a problem since I was a … - umm when I was in the choir I had a number of … solos. *I'm* not trying to show off or anything just showing relevant experience. so it's not a problem for me at all. and obviously I was - I've been … a member of umm … various debate teams while I was at college as well. … and that's arguing in public anyway so

11. Yeah … very confident. I mean I'd have to handle it umm anyway in my choices in career so … yeah [3 sec.] definitely.

12. Umm I - I - I've … told it's a tutoring job. I've told it's more than one person. I know - I - I've gathered from what I've been told that it's more than one person. just how … big - with it - is it like classes? /Interviewer/ it is cl - that's fine. /Interviewer/ oh that's good yeah. /Interviewer/ that's good. [3 sec.] yeah. so I yeah. /Interviewer/ *is* umm [2 sec.] umm is umm - just … basically … how - how would the umm - the … - the running of the lessons … umm take place? how would - how … - how would the /Interviewer/ <yeah> the grammar yeah. /Interviewer/ pronunciations /Interviewer/ <mhm, okay, yeah> umm I - I'm sorry how many - how many hours a week as well? *is it* /Interviewer/ four hours that's fine yeah. /Interviewer/ okay /Interviewer/ that's fine.

I 39f

Sex: female
Age: 21
Origin: Windsor, GB

1. Okay. I'm - I was … born in … umm … Ascot which is near to Windsor, umm and I've lived pretty much my whole life in Windsor, [laughs slightly] umm … I visited … three schools there, umm … yeah in Windsor we have a … three school umm system. so the first school until you're nine years old, then umm a middle school until thirteen and then a high school … umm which I stayed at to do my A-levels as well, … and I took A-levels in English literature … umm history … French and German, … and I … then deci - umm took the decision to study in Cardiff, umm … where I've studied now for the last two years, … umm … doing German and English literature, … umm … yeah and now I'm out here in Passau [laughs] as part of my degree course.

2. Umm [2 sec.] well umm … all - I mean all of us … doing German have to … umm do either a semester or two semesters out here … and then umm … yeah we had a choice of about eight places or so … umm to study in and … I *chose* … Passau [laughs] *just* … - yeah I … did a bit of research on it and it … *yeah suited me I think*

3. [2 sec.] umm … well yeah hopefully umm … and most importantly umm English literature. umm [2 sec.] and - and umm … yeah also in German we study umm a lot about grammar and umm … yeah *how* … *to apply it to language and* [3 sec.] but I - I've never done anything … like teaching before *so* … it would be a new experience for me [laughs slightly]

4. [3 sec.] Oh umm [laughs slightly] umm [3 sec.] yeah I - I like to think that I'm … quite patient with people so umm … I'd be able to … sit down with them and help them work through their problems. … umm [2 sec.] yeah and I - I like to … see other people achieve things and … that would make me ever so proud if I had then helped them to achieve that. … *so* … [laughs slightly]

5. Umm [2 sec.] strengths I'd have to say I was … very hard working … umm I always have been [laughs slightly] umm … I'm also very organized, … umm … yeah umm *I did* lots and lots of gymnastics as a

child so I always had to fit in my homework ... in ... certain days and certain times so that's made me ... very very organized. ... umm ... umm weaknesses? umm [3 sec.] *yeah I s - ...* umm ... *I suppose* yeah sometimes [2 sec.] I ... let myself umm be put down too easily by criticism. ... and ... sometimes I work a little bit too hard [laughs] at what I'm doing and don't give myself enough of a break. ... I always try and keep a ... good balance

6. [3 sec.] umm [2 sec.] I *suppose* it's just gonna be such a - a new experience to do and umm ... yeah be umm ... really good to ... help other people with their ... learning ... in English and ... yeah I know that ... lots of people here have helped me already to ... improve my German and ... yeah if I can then ... give ... other students the chance to improve their English [2 sec.] /Interviewer/ really good /Interviewer/ umm I don't really know ... umm ... a lot about what it ... well entails [laughs slightly] *I'm not really too sure.*

7. ... umm ... I suppose ... a lot of the time it depends on the task that we're doing but umm ... certainly ... yes it's much much easier to work in a group and to work through problems and ... umm other people always have a different idea to you and if you can ... put that all together then you ... get a very interesting outcome to a question. ... *mhm*

8. Yeah [laughs] ... that - that's obviously ... something that you have to ... work through umm ... persevere I guess umm [2 sec.] *umm* yeah not - not pressure them too hard but then ... also not *sort of* delineate too far from the task that ... you've got ahead of you and *umm* try and keep them on track with what they're meant to be learning but ... maybe try and make the lesson a bit more fun and ... get them to interact with each other and ... try and put a smile back on their face in some way [laughs slightly]

9. Umm [laughs slightly] ... yeah sometimes I do let it get me down umm [3 sec.] yeah you have to - to ... take - take in the comments and umm ... work from them and try and improve what you've been doing

10. Yeah I participated in a public speaking competition umm in school when I was in the sixth form, ... umm ... yeah we had to - umm we were in a group of three or so and we had to ... discuss ... ideas and ... present them individually ... before ... a ... large hall of people. [laughs slightly]

11. I hope so yes. [laughs slightly]
12. ... umm ... yeah how ... big are the groups that ... we'd be teaching? /Interviewer/ oh okay. [2 sec.] that's quite nice size then. okay. /Interviewer/ umm [5 sec.] *I think umm* ... [laughs] /Interviewer/ *I think that*'s *about* (*everything*) /Interviewer/ okay

I 40f

Sex: female
Age: 20
Origin: Sheffield, GB

1. Okay ... umm ... I come from ... Sheffield, which is in middle England ... umm ... and ... I study German and Spanish, ... so ... here I'm spending half a year ... - or one semester here ... and ... I have to study ... German language classes, ... German literature ... so ... basically just ... lots of German ... *courses*, ... umm ... and then I have to go to Spain ... next semester, ... to study Spanish.

2. Umm [2 sec.] well German was my favourite ... subject at school, ... so ... umm I decided to do it at university, and then ... umm ... yeah I - I really enjoy speaking languages so ... yeah ... *I decided to ... study German*, and ... (*and it says*) - you have to - you have to come ... umm ... half a year abroad or a year abroad when you study *German*.

3. Umm ... as a tutor? umm [2 sec.] it will probably - it will give me ... umm ... experience of teaching, ... I'd maybe ... like to become a teacher after university, ... umm ... I'm not really sure exactly what ... - what I ... get for it but

4. Umm ... with the English teaching? /Interviewer/ yeah umm [2 sec.] help me [2 sec.] - yeah it'll give me experience of teaching, umm ... *in front of* ... a class, ... umm communication skills, ... I mean maybe ... give me confidence umm ... by having to speak umm - teach people, [3 sec.] /Interviewer/ umm [2 sec.] what ...? /Interviewer/ umm [3 sec.] umm I - I - I've worked with people a lot so ... I guess that will help, ... umm ... I've never done any teaching or anything but [2 sec.] yeah

5. ... umm [laughs slightly] ... my strengths I'd say ... umm [5 sec.] I'm friendly [laughs slightly] ... umm [2 sec.] and [2 sec.] I like to ... learn a lot more and experience things, ... umm [3 sec.] yeah I don't really know. [laughs slightly] umm [5 sec.] umm [2 sec.] (hey) I can be quite shy sometimes, I suppose that can be a weakness ... umm [4 sec.] and [3 sec.] *I ... don't ... I don't* really know. [laughs slightly]

6. ... umm [2 sec.] yeah I'm interested in ... umm... meeting German students, ... umm ... and be able to ... umm ... yeah have the experience of teaching them, ... umm [4 sec.] and yeah just communicating with

them, [4 sec.] /Interviewer/ umm [3 sec.] I - there's not really anything least.

7. Umm ... I'd say both. sometimes I like ... umm working in groups, ... and sharing ideas ... umm but then sometimes ... I just like to get on with something and do it myself, ... it depends *what* the work is.

8. Umm ... I'd try talking to them and explaining ... umm ... that they're here to learn, and ... hopefully they'll ... understand me and *listen to me* [laughs slightly]

9. Mhm ... umm ... I suppose ... don't take it too personally, ... umm there's gon - there's going to be criticism because ... not everyone is gonna agree with everything I say, ... so ... I suppose just ... yeah listen to what they say and try and improve ... if I made a mistake, ... but not take it too ... - too hard.

10. Umm ... only ... by doing umm presentations in class ... and nothing ... - nothing really.

11. Umm ... yeah I think so. ... mhm. I hope so.

12. Okay umm ... yeah what - I don't really ... know exactly what it - what it is? umm ... where are we teaching the class or? ... a whole class? /Interviewer/ <okay, mhm> and ... do ... - do ... they have work already? ... it's a programme I follow or? /Interviewer/ <mhm, okay> and how often? /Interviewer/ <mhm, okay> okay. ... but you have to do four hours? ... a week. ... and is that in one day or different days? /Interviewer/ <okay> /Interviewer/ umm ... [laughs slightly] I don't think so ... *no* /Interviewer/ okay

Ingram Content Group UK Ltd.
Milton Keynes UK
UKHW041450110423
419975UK00004B/36

9 783631 654026